Colin Robson

# Experiment, Design and Statistics in Psychology

## Third Edition

PENGUIN BOOKS

PENGUIN BOOKS

Published by the Penguin Group
Penguin Books Ltd, 27 Wrights Lane, London W8 5TZ, England
Penguin Books USA Inc., 375 Hudson Street, New York, New York 10014, USA
Penguin Books Australia Ltd, Ringwood, Victoria, Australia
Penguin Books Canada Ltd, 10 Alcorn Avenue, Toronto, Ontario, Canada M4V 3B2
Penguin Books (NZ) Ltd, 182–190 Wairau Road, Auckland 10, New Zealand

Penguin Books Ltd, Registered Offices: Harmondsworth, Middlesex, England

First published in Penguin Books 1973
Second edition 1983
Reprinted in Pelican Books 1985
Third edition published in Penguin Books 1994

10 9 8 7 6 5 4 3 2

Typeset by Datix International Limited, Bungay, Suffolk
Printed in England by Clays Ltd, St Ives plc
Filmset in Monophoto Times and Helvetica

*To my wife*

# Contents

# How to select a test

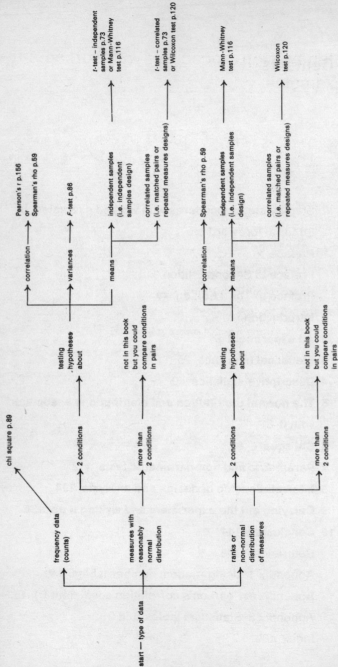

# Step-by-step procedures with worked examples

# Editorial foreword

There are basic skills which are essential for progress in a variety of subjects, but which often prove to be stumbling blocks for people who otherwise have the necessary ability and motivation. Particularly is this true of various branches of mathematics, especially statistics. Many pure and applied scientists, and non-scientists too, need to have a working knowledge of statistics, and in a large number of cases they develop a block against the subject. A common reaction is to argue that the actual work can be left to the professional statisticians 'as long as I know where to go for help'. This is rather like arguing 'I need not make my car safe because I know where to go for first aid.' The planning of one's own work, and one's appraisal of other people's, is immeasurably improved by *first hand* experience of statistical techniques.

I did not think it was possible to write an introduction to statistics which was postively entertaining, but Colin Robson has succeeded. He is a psychologist and the book is a result of courses given to psychology students, but the techniques which he teaches are the basic ones used in a variety of disciplines. Especially important is the way the author leads the reader into working out examples, because statistics is one of those subjects in which the learner can develop insight as a result of practice. Familiarity becomes a pretty good substitute for a knowledge of the underlying mathematics.

People who understand the mathematics but can also teach the techniques in a simple way are difficult to find. Colin Robson says he is not a Statistician (with a capital S). He is, however, a very good teacher.

B.M.F.

# Preface

For a number of years I have lectured on summer courses in experimental psychology, statistics and experimental design at the University of London for external students registered for degrees in psychology. Students on these courses were of extremely varied mathematical background which meant that, if all were to follow the work in statistics, little beyond elementary algebra could be assumed. The core of this book consists of material from lectures and hand-outs presented for these courses. It has been pretty well pre-tested in that the students on these courses were excellent at giving feedback if a particular approach was unclear. While a lot of ground is covered in a relatively small number of words, many of the basic concepts are introduced and reintroduced at several points in the book. This redundancy, which springs from the fact that the material was originally intended for aural consumption, is, I hope, helpful rather than the converse. Similarly, no attempt has been made to alter the informal style in which the material was originally presented.

I am not a statistician, as may perhaps be revealed to any of that breed who read this. However, I have had a good deal of enjoyment in initiating students – particularly those who shy away from anything mathematical and have to be handled with a very loose rein – into the mysteries and delights of designing and analysing experiments.

I am indebted to the literary executor of the late Sir Ronald A. Fisher, F.R.S., to Dr Frank Yates, F.R.S., and to Oliver & Boyd, Edinburgh, for permission to reprint Table 33 from their book *Statistical Tables for Biological, Agricultural and Medical Research*.

Finally, I would like to thank the students mentioned above, my wife for her attempts to tame my written style, and Pat Needham and Susan Moorhouse for expert and speedy assistance with typing.

Colin Robson
1973

# Preface to Second Edition

Since preparing the first edition of this book I have gained further experience in teaching the introductory statistics and experimental design course, mainly with students on the Behavioural Sciences degree at Huddersfield Polytechnic. They have been no less vociferous than the external psychology degree students of London University in indicating any lack of clarity and their resulting confusion. The modifications in this second edition are largely resulting from this interaction.

In particular I am now no longer persuaded by statisticians' arguments as to the superiority of Kendall's tau over Spearman's rho and feel that the computational simplicity of the latter gives it the edge. Pearson's correlation coefficient is covered in an Appendix as it figures in several introductory syllabuses and is useful in introducing ideas needed in more advanced work.

The example used to introduce basic notions about experiments has been brought up-to-date and there is a somewhat more serious attempt to explain the concept of probability. Otherwise the basic approach in the first edition has been retained. I have been very grateful for the feedback I have received both face to face and in written form. Some modifications arise from such comments although I have resisted advice that the book might concern itself more with issues to do with tests and testing, with reliability, validity etc., primarily to keep it as slim as possible.

Much of the drudgery associated with computing, say, a $t$-test, is removed by using the calculator and I would urge all those using this book not only to get a calculator but also to acquire some facility in its use. Given the rapid changes in this area it is not very helpful to recommend specific models. A square root and a memory function are useful but I feel that starting out by using the more complex programmable calculators tends to defeat the object of understanding something of the basis of the various tests. Given that understanding there is, of course, a lot to be said for using more powerful machines. Microcomputers have much to offer in this connection and the reader may be interested to know that the statistical tests covered in this book, together with more complex tests, are incorporated in the SUPASTAT programs developed by one of my colleagues for use on the 380 Z and Apple microcomputers.

Colin Robson
1983

# Preface to Third Edition

The continuing positive response to the second edition of this text might be seen as an excuse for leaving well alone. However, the world changes and so does the context in which the continually increasing numbers of psychology students first come into contact with the requirement to design and analyse experiments. I have also realized that, through my teaching and research experiences of the last decade, I too have changed somewhat in my appreciation of the role and position of experimentation (strictly speaking, that of 'true' or 'randomized' experimentation) in psychology and other sciences involving the study of people. Rather than seeing it as *the* strategy to use, I now look upon it much more as one of a range of possible approaches; as a strategy with undoubted strengths, but also with major weaknesses and limitations in its use. Hence a somewhat more critical approach to the virtues and usefulness of doing experiments has been taken in this edition.

Nevertheless, I remain totally convinced that the student of psychology must acquire not only some understanding of the place of experimental work in the discipline, but also skills in the design, carrying out, analysis and interpretation of such experiments. This text, as in the earlier editions, seeks to 'engage' students in this task. The treatment is deliberately simple without, I hope, appearing condescending. Many potential qualifications and amplifications have been omitted in the cause of not obscuring the main argument. The text has been fully revised with a view to simplifying wherever this seems feasible and helpful, and amplifying where necessary.

One important contextual change is the ready availability for microcomputers of several software packages for the statistical analysis of data. Notwithstanding this, I believe that there is virtue in the student on the *introductory* course in this area not only seeing the statistical formulae used and achieving at least an intuitive understanding of their underlying rationale, but also actually working through at least some of the analyses with data that they have collected. My preference is to make the transition to the use of statistical packages also as part of the introductory course to avoid the danger of the 'statistically challenged' student (who is also likely to be 'computer challenged') persevering with hard-won prowess at hand-calculating *t*-tests and the like. Hence I have continued with the 'step-by-step procedures' and 'worked example' approaches for statistical tests of earlier editions with the expectation that, where facilities are available, tutors will facilitate the transition to use of computer packages as and when they judge appropriate.

I have followed the increasingly common usage whereby those who take part in the experiment are referred to as 'participants' rather than as 'subjects'. While this might smack of pandering to political correctness, the switch is, I feel, of some importance. Asking people to participate in something is different from 'subjecting' them to it. Thinking in these terms may help us to avoid some of the excesses which can arise from the unequal power relationship of experimenter and experimented-upon.

The nature of the text will make it clear that I believe in experimental design and statistics being taught together, preferably in a course which also incorporates the practical work itself. In this connection I would like to commend the recently published *BPS Manual of Psychology Practicals*\* which provides a useful complementary source of practical exercises usable at different levels. I would also like to thank colleagues at Huddersfield and in particular the Behavioural Sciences students who continue to help in my education as we jointly come to terms with modularization, semesterization and learning outcomes. I am also grateful to the many teachers, lecturers and students from other institutions who have

\*McIlveen, R., Higgins, L., Wadeley, A. and Humphreys, P. (1992), *BPS Manual of Psychology Practicals: Experiment, observation and correlation*, British Psychological Society.

provided invaluable feedback through their puzzlement or appreciation.

Colin Robson
1993

*Note to the 1995 reprint:* The opportunity has been taken to simplify the treatment of chi square $2 \times 2$ contingency tables (Chapter 6) by omitting 'Yates's correction'. This is now regarded in statistical circles as both theoretically unsound and showing a conservative bias. I am grateful to Professor Richardson in the Department of Human Sciences, Brunel University, for continuing my education. A rationale is provided in Richardson, J. T. E. (1990), 'Variants of Chi-square for $2 \times 2$ Contingency Tables', *British Journal of Statistical and Mathematical Psychology*, vol. 43, pp. 309–26.

Colin Robson
1995

# 1 Introduction

## What this book tries to do

My aim is to help you to design, carry out, analyse and interpret simple experiments. The focus is on the use of the experimental approach when studying people and their ways, particularly as carried out by psychologists – although the same principles apply to experiments carried out by other social or behavioural scientists, and professionals in applied fields such as education, social services or health care. As far as statistics and statistical tests are concerned, the book is a 'cook-book'. It has been designed to guide you to the right recipe – the statistical test appropriate to the problem – and then carry you through the steps of the recipe with a maximum of detail. The intention is not to train statisticians, but to give people doing simple experiments a range of useful statistical tools. Formulae are not derived, and the only mathematical requirement is some elementary algebra, together with the ability to substitute numbers into formulae. As mentioned in the preface to this edition, it is now possible to use software available on most microcomputers to actually carry out the computation. If you have a large amount of data only a masochist would do the analysis by hand. However, it does help to know what you are doing and there is much to be said for carrying out the analysis of simple experiments with relatively small amounts of data 'by hand' (in practice this means using a simple electronic calculator to do the multiplying, squaring, etc.).

However, the book is not just a 'cook-book'. Apart from the fact that such a compendium of statistical recipes would be deadly boring and hardly likely to kindle any flames of interest or enthusiasm, it would not be able to fulfil the stated aim of the book. If you are to select a particular statistical test, you need to appreciate what the test is capable of doing, why it is that that particular test is appropriate and others are not. In order to achieve this, some kind of understanding, even if only at an intuitive level, is essential. Hence an attempt is made to talk around and lead up to the tests in such a way that that kind of understanding has a chance to develop.

There are many sad stories of students, burning to carry out an experimental project, who end up with a completely unanalysable mishmash of data. They wanted to get on with it and thought that they could leave thoughts of analysis until after the experiment. They were wrong. Statistical analysis and experimental design must be considered together and, whilst there are broad principles of experimental design which will be covered, they cannot easily be reduced to recipes guaranteed for every eventuality.

Using statistics is no insurance against producing rubbish. Badly used, misapplied statistics simply allow one to produce quantitative rubbish rather than qualitative rubbish.

## Limitations of the book

Do not get the impression that all the techniques of statistical analysis are to be laid at your feet in the next chapters. This is not the case. You will be given a severely limited range of techniques. What I do hope, however, is that you will be able to take research questions that you are interested in and turn them into simple experiments which can be analysed meaningfully by one or more tests out of this repertoire.

This will not always be possible and you may well find that in trying to fit your experiment into the strait-jacket of these techniques, so much violence is done to the original idea that it is not worth doing.

The intention is that you should be able to recognize situations like this. Your strategy then is to try to approach the research question from a different direction. It may be that, for one or more of several possible reasons, your question is just not amenable to dealing with by an experiment. We will see later in the chapter that while there are very good reasons for seeking to use experimental approaches, it does require rather special circumstances for this to be a sensible strategy. And even if an experiment were sensible, it may well be that your questions call for more complex designs or statistical analyses than those covered here. However, do not be discouraged; it is surprising how many interesting questions can be investigated in simply designed experiments for which the simple designs and straightforward statistical tests described here are adequate and appropriate.

## Requirements from the reader

The main requirements, virtually the only requirement, is that *you should want to do experiments.* If you are certain that you don't want to do experiments then you are wasting your time reading this book and should find a more profitable way of spending your time. It is true that a knowledge of statistics and experimental design enables one to understand and evaluate other people's experiments, and this should come as a bonus from reading the book. But even if that is your aim, the experience of having carried out your own experiments will stand you in good stead.

This book is addressed directly to the reader who wants to experiment but doesn't know how to go about it (including those who have started out with that intention but have got confused or dispirited). My interest and sympathies lie with you and your concerns. If you already have a specific problem or question that you would like to turn into an experiment, well and good. It will not be a bad thing for you to go through, considering each of the approaches discussed in turn to see whether it fits in with your research question. If you do not have a problem, no need to worry. Providing you keep your eyes and ears open and start thinking 'experimentally' you will be assailed at each and every turn by problems that might form the basis of interesting experiments. If, by the time you have reached the end of the book, you are still keen but remain without such a problem, the last chapter suggests some of the things that you might do about it.

## What is an experiment anyway?

In everyday use the terms 'experiment' and 'experimental' are used very generally to refer to some kind of trial or investigation. Here, the meaning is much more specific.

In the simplest experiment, one investigates the relationship between two things by deliberately producing a change in one of them and looking at, observing, the change in the other. These 'things' in which change takes place are called **variables**.

The variable which we, as experimenters, are directly manipulating is called the **independent variable**. The variable in which we are looking for any consequent changes is called the **dependent variable**. The independent variable is so-called because it is independent of what the participants in the experiment actually do (it is predetermined by the experimenter). The dependent variable is so-called because changes in it are (potentially, at least) dependent on changes in the independent variable. To take an example: suppose that one is interested in the effect of financial reward on the performance of some complex task. An experiment could be devised where the independent variable would be the amount of money given, and the dependent variable some measure of the performance of the task, for example, the number of errors made.

A second important feature of the experiment is that the experimenter not only deliberately manipulates the independent variable and looks for possible changes on the dependent variable, but also seeks to control other variables so that they do not affect the outcome. Suppose that the problem or research question is concerned with the relative effectiveness of lectures given in the early morning or late afternoon. In this case the independent variable is the time of the lectures, and the dependent variable some measure of the effectiveness of the lectures. This measure might, for instance, be the amount of information remembered about the lectures. There are many other things which might affect the amount remembered, apart from the time of the lecture. The students or the lecturer might be different (different actual people or different in terms of their performance – are you as alert in the afternoons as in the mornings?). Or the material of the lecture. Or the lecture room. Or the conditions in the room. Or what happened in the hour before the lecture. One could go on, and on, and on . . . What we are saying here is that there are other variables apart from the independent variable, which might affect the dependent variable. Providing experimenters have sufficient patience, cunning and ingenuity, they can arrange to control all these other variables in such a way that they will not affect the assessment of the relationship between the independent and dependent variable.

The experiment is not limited to a consideration of a single, independent variable and its possible effects on a single dependent variable. Most published experiments involve the manipulation of several independent variables, and there is a trend towards studies with more than one dependent variable. However, such studies, to be adequately analysed, tend to involve complex statistical techniques which are beyond the range of the introductory text.

## The big advantage of experiments

In a well-designed experiment where adequate control measures have been taken against other variables, there is an inherent plausibility to the claim that changes observed in the dependent variable have been *caused* by your manipulation of the independent variable. This ability of the experiment to get at causal relationships is its big advantage over other approaches.

With non-experimental approaches, such as the typical survey, claims about causality are more difficult to substantiate. In a situation where many variables are free to vary, you can never be sure that changes in one particular variable occur as a result of changes in a second particular variable. It is always possible that a third variable is causally related to both of the first two and has produced the relationship observed between them. For example, an observational study of the 'Trooping of the Colour' ceremony over a number of years could well demonstrate a strong relationship between the softness of the tar on the parade ground and the number of guardsmen fainting on parade. Any direct causal relationship, such as the poor chaps being overcome by noxious fumes from the tar, appears to be highly unlikely and I would surmise (although I have not tested this) that an actual experiment would fail to demonstrate any relationship. The obvious causal link is, of

5

course, that of temperature. The rising temperature causes both the tar to soften and the guardsmen to faint.

A more serious example is the relationship found by several surveys between smoking and lung cancer. For ethical reasons no actual experiments have been carried out with humans to investigate this link (see p. 94 for further discussion). Hence it is possible that, although there is a strong relationship between smoking and cancer, smoking may not be the cause of cancer. The cause may be, for example, in some personality or other psychological characteristics which predispose to both smoking and cancer.

Nevertheless, non-experimental studies do have an important part to play in investigations, psychological or otherwise. There are many situations, other than the smoking and lung cancer one, where direct experimentation is not possible. Perfectly respectable sciences such as astronomy and geology have to rely almost exclusively on direct observation without the possiblity of the active manipulation of an independent variable required for an experiment. Working with humans, and indeed with other animals, there are ethical reasons why variables involving painful stimuli, surgical operations and so on, should not be manipulated, and here non-experimental studies may well be preferable.

There are also strong arguments for conducting at least the initial stages of investigation into an area in an open-ended exploratory fashion, even when experimentation is feasible. In this way it is possible to get some idea of which variables are most important. The experiment is a very precise tool. As experimenter you are, as it were, putting your bets on a particular independent variable and a particular dependent variable as the ones likely to be causally related. Even in more complex experiments you are restricted to just a few of the many possible variables that you might choose. For the choice of an experiment to be a sensible strategy you need to have a justified confidence in your choice of variables, obtained either from previous work carried out by others or by exploratory work of your own.

## Some difficulties with experiments

The preceding paragraphs make it clear that there are some situations and research problems where it may not be feasible nor appropriate to carry out an experiment. For some, the time may not yet be ripe in that insufficient is known to devise a sensible design. For others, such as the lung cancer example, experiments are effectively ruled out in principle.

There are other difficulties. A common criticism of experiments is that they are artificial and over-simplified. To fulfil the requirements of control of variables you may be in danger of throwing away the baby with the bath-water. Suppose you start out with a research question on some aspect of car-driving behaviour. The process of designing an experiment, and in particular the need to control the many variables encountered in 'real' driving on the open road, may well lead you to end up with a study of persons pushing buttons in a laboratory cubicle in reponse to a flashing light.

The mere fact that an experiment is typically a rather special event taking place in a special place may mean that what is found out is of limited generality. Human participants bring their expectations and perceptions into this situation; they may be seeking to please the experimenter or the reverse. The effects of the experimenters' own expectancies on the behaviour of participants have been extensively researched. Barber (1976) provides a balanced account of these, and other, potential pitfalls.

## Experiments and laboratories

Traditionally, experiments take place in laboratories. The prime reason for this is that it helps in controlling variables. The use of specialized equipment, such as the tachistoscope, is essentially so that the experimenter can obtain very precise control over what happens to participants. However, there is no iron law that says that experiments must take place in laboratories, and for certain types of question so-called 'field' experiments may well be preferable. Remember that the central feature of the experiment is the deliberate manipulation of some variable. The ingenious experimenter may well find ways of setting this up in a school, hospital ward, pub or wherever. Some lack of control over variables is probably inevitable but the increased naturalness of the setting may well reap considerable benefits.

## A warning

Finally, a warning against over-optimism, and against the rejection or devaluing of findings and evidence from non-experimental approaches. There was a wave of enthusiasm for experimentation in education in the 1920s. This was followed by a wave of pessimism and disillusionment. The advocates of experimentation assumed that progress in teaching methods had been slow just because there had been little or no experimentation. When their experiments proved to be tedious, equivocal, difficult to replicate (i.e. for their findings to be supported when the study was repeated) and to accord with common sense, then disillusionment and rejection of experimentation took place.

The justification for the experimental method is not as a panacea to be used in all situations to seek answers for all problems. It is that when questions amenable to experimental 'attack' can be devised, it is the simplest and most straightforward method we know for getting at cause and effect relationships.

# 2 An experiment

## From vague thoughts to specific plans

This chapter covers the kinds of steps you need to make in developing a simple experimental design. You may have problems or questions of your own which you would like to turn into actual experiments. If so, good. Or you may have a topic given to you by someone else. Wherever the idea comes from there will be a need to move from something which is vague, woolly and ill-formulated to a specific plan of action.

Suppose one is interested in absent-mindedness; a topic which is familiar enough but which has, until recently, been largely neglected by the psychologist. The interested reader is referred to Baddeley (1981) who discusses work which he and others have done in this area as examples of studies of the cognitive psychology of everyday life.

The first step in designing an experiment is to try to get a reasonably explicit statement of the problem with which you are trying to deal. What is meant by absent-mindedness? It appears to be connected with not remembering to do something. I am reminded of a former colleague who would probably win prizes for absent-mindedness. While this showed itself in a variety of ways, his particular speciality lay in keys and cheque-books which were regularly mislaid: he would forget to bring keys with him when leaving the house or he would leave his cheque-book on the desk after using it, where it would disappear under a pile of papers. This was not a case of someone poor at either remembering or recall of material in the usual sense. Certainly he had an almost encyclopaedic knowledge of the published research in his area of specialism.

A possible design strategy might be to seek to relate these phenomena to some theory. Those with a Freudian leaning might see significance in the fact that it is keys and cheque-books which are forgotten. Seductive as such musings might be, Freud's concepts have proved notoriously difficult to translate into worthwhile experiments (whether this reveals shortcomings in Freudian theory or in the use of experimental approaches when seeking to understand humans is a separate issue which could well form the basis of another book). A more mundane approach, but probably more productive for the experimentalist, and perhaps more likely to lead to practical suggestions for dealing with the absent-mindedness, might be to analyse in more detail the circumstances in which the forgetting takes place. What might well be involved here is him not giving himself a cue to check something at a particular time. Is his difficulty that of checking that he has his key when leaving the house? And is this 'omitting to check' a common feature in cases of absent-mindedness?

Clearly one could move from this kind of anecdotal musing to design an experiment where one or more aspects of remembering to check something at a particular time are tested. This is the approach taken by Baddeley and his colleagues in a variety of tasks. These include having people return postcards to them at specified dates after they had been given them, and a simulation of the pill-taking regime of 'four times a day after meals' where volunteers had to press a button on a modified watch at four specified times each day.

However, there may be other facets of absent-mindedness exemplified by going to a café for a cup of tea and asking for a newspaper (or going to a newsagent and asking for a cup of coffee), as I have done on more than one occasion. This aspect was investigated by a group of students from Bexhill Sixth Form College in connection with a BBC television series 'Young Scientist of the Year' (further details are given in Baddeley, 1981). Their initial investigations of such 'slips of action' (other examples being answering the telephone by giving an address and trying to put on tights when wearing slippers) showed that there were quite considerable differences between individuals in the extent to which they reported such things as happening to them, and that the slips tended to occur when trying to perform a routine activity at the same time as doing something else.

The strategy of the Bexhill sixth-formers was to isolate two 'extreme' groups of people; one group who reported that they had no slips of this kind, and a second group who reported a lot of such slips. These two groups then participated in experimental situations where they had to perform two tasks at the same time.

This process of refining and clarifying the problem you are working on calls for a mixture of common sense and clear thinking. However, there is a quite substantial amount of jargon (or to put it more positively, technical language) associated with the design of experiments which you need to be familiar with – if only so that you can understand accounts of experiments, and communicate what you have done to others. Some of the important terms you need to know are covered in the rest of this chapter and the next one.

## Independent and dependent variables

The terms 'independent variable' and 'dependent variable' were introduced on p. 4 when discussing what is meant by an experiment. However, it will do no harm to go through this again here.

What we are doing in a simple experiment is trying to observe the relationship between two variables. The variable which the experimenter manipulates is called the **independent variable** (this is often simply abbreviated as IV). The IV here is concerned with some aspect of absent-mindedness. In the design of the experiment we are going to have to be very clear as to what we mean by this – see the discussion below on 'operational definitions'.

You should note that the independent variable is being manipulated here by the way in which the experimenter selects the groups taking part in the experiment – the two extreme groups of 'high' and 'low' absent-mindedness. It would be difficult to directly manipulate the degree to which a particular individual is absent-minded. A similar, and very common, example occurs in experiments looking at gender differences where the experimenter selects female and male groups. This type of 'manipulation by selection' leads to complications in the interpretation of the results of the experiment, discussed in Chapter 8 (p. 132). There are, however, many situations where it is perfectly feasible to manipulate the independent variable directly by, for example, altering the type of material presented or in some other way changing the type of experience or situation for different groups.

The variable which is observed in order to see whether changes in the IV have any effect on it is known as the **dependent variable** (also commonly found in abbreviated form as DV). Here the DV is some aspect of performance of the tasks. Again this has to be very carefully defined – see the discussion below on 'operational definitions'.

In psychological experiments the independent variable is very often a stimulus variable (e.g. the type of material to be learned, the brightness of a light, exposure-time of a word, etc.): that is, in general, the **input** to the person taking part. An important exception to this has already been noted. This is when the independent variable is associated with a feature of the people taking part in the experiment (e.g. 'male' or 'female'). The dependent variable is almost always a response variable (time taken to make a response, strength of response, number of responses, etc.): that is, in general, the **output** from the persons taking part.

## Qualitative and quantitative variables

Fairly obviously, a 'variable' is something which can vary. In other words, it can take on different values or levels. For instance, if the dependent variable is the number of errors made this might take on just about any whole number (integral) value. In an experiment where we are considering how problem-solving varies with age, the dependent variable would be age, and the values or levels of the variable used might be 4 years, 6 years, 8 years, 10 years, etc. Variables expressed in numbers in this way are referred to as quantitative variables. Dependent variables are almost always quantitative (if one includes in this category simple counts as to how many times a particular thing occurs) as this then opens the possibility of statistical analysis, which is regarded by conventional experimentalists as central to their approach.

The independent variable is, however, quite commonly qualitative rather than quantitative, as in the example of the use of gender as an independent variable. Here, any assignment of numbers such as 'female = 1' and 'male = 2' (which may be done, for example, in coding survey responses) is purely arbitrary. In our 'absent-mindedness' example the two values of the independent variable are effectively 'high absent-mindedness' and 'low absent-mindedness'. While they are derived from numerical values they are in fact treated qualitatively rather than quantitatively.

## Experimental conditions

The values of the IV ('high absent-mindedness' and 'low absent-mindedness') are commonly called the **experimental conditions**. (You may also find them referred to as 'treatment conditions'.) In this experiment, and in almost all the other experiments considered in this book, we will deal with just two values of the IV (i.e., two experimental conditions). This is partly because the statistical techniques that will be covered can only deal with two conditions at a time. However, keeping within these limits, it is possible to answer a very large number of experimental problems. There are techniques for dealing with more than two conditions at a time, and these are covered in more advanced texts. Another possibility is to deal with more complicated experimental designs by considering the values of the independent variable two at a time. This kind of piecemeal approach is not recommended as it can throw away many of the advantages of using more complex designs.

## Operational definitions

An **operational definition** is stated in terms of the steps or operations that have to be carried out in observing or measuring whatever it is that is being defined. Before we can make an idea for the experiment into an actual experiment that we can carry out, we must define our independent and dependent variables in this way.

In considering the independent variable and the specific experimental conditions (levels or values of the IV) we need to ask ourselves exactly what we mean. What aspect of 'absent-mindedness' are we focusing on, and what is 'low absent-mindedness' and 'high absent-mindedness'? Here the procedure (i.e. the steps or operations followed) was to ask for recording of the absent-minded 'slips' over a four-week period. Those reporting no instances over the period were assigned to the 'low absent-mindedness' group; those reporting more than eight to the 'high absent-mindedness' group.

As far as the dependent variable was concerned the exact nature of the two tasks had to be specified, together with exactly what was to be measured. The two tasks were backward counting in threes from a specified number and mirror-drawing. The latter, if you are not familiar with it, is a common laboratory task involving tracing around the outline of a star with the tracing hand only visible through a mirror – a surprisingly difficult and frustrating task. The measure in the first task was the number of items counted in a specified time and in the second task the time taken to complete the maze.

It is only when we have precisely defined the variables that the experiment can be carried out. Equally important, it is essential that we define the terms in this exact way so that some later worker, coming along and seeing our results, being interested in them or perhaps even disbelieving them, will then be able to set up an exact replica of our experiment in order to check on the result we have obtained.

This is called **replication** of the experiment. While it may not seem a particularly exciting or interesting task it is an important one and should probably take place much more frequently than it does currently in psychological and other research involving people. We may be building our disciplines on shaky foundations. For example, a very widely quoted and influential study 'Pygmalion in the Classroom' by Rosenthal (who has carried out much of the work on 'experimenter expectancy' effects referred to on p. 136) showed that teachers' expectations of children's performance, artificially manipulated in the experiment, brought that performance up to the expectations. Shipman (1988) points out that several attempts to replicate these 'findings' have been unsuccessful. Similarly, Baddeley notes with regret that the particular findings of the 'Bexhill' study have, to date, proved impossible to replicate. Perhaps we can leave further studies in this area as a challenge to the reader.

## Subjects or participants?

The convention has been that those taking part in an experiment are referred to as **subjects**. The symbol $S$ is used to indicate a subject (but it is sometimes used in statistics to stand for other things – so beware). The use of the term 'subject' is now criticized by some as indicating an inappropriate kind of relationship – being the 'subject of investigation' or 'subject to the control of the experimenter'. It could be argued that this is in fact a fair description of the power relationships in the experimental situation, but I have to admit that once sensitized to such issues I now prefer the term **participant** – i.e. someone taking part in the experiment. Given that the British Psychological Society now uses this terminology in its 'Ethical Principles for Conducting Research with Human Participants' (BPS, 1993) I propose to make the switch to 'participant' in this text (sorry that it is longer than 'subject'; and, unfortunately, the corresponding symbol $P$ can also stand for other things in statistics).

## Samples and populations

When carrying out an experiment the usual hope and intention is to try to find out something of relevance and applicability beyond the specific group of participants involved on a particular day in a particular place using particular equipment and materials. Mention has already been made of the necessary artificiality of much laboratory work which calls into question its relevance to real world, non-laboratory settings. In practice, judgements are made about wider applicability in terms of plausibility. Is this the kind of finding likely to have been different if the study had been carried out in Stockport or Stockholm rather than in Stevenage? In summer as against winter; or using flash cards instead of a tachistoscope? Such questions can be addressed directly by seeking to replicate the findings and establishing how robust they are.

However, a particular form of reasoning is commonly used in experimentation and depends on the notion of samples and populations. Specifically, if we can show that in carrying out an experiment we are dealing with a sample which is representative of a certain known population, then it is possible for us to generalize with a degree of confidence from the specific sample to the population which it represents. Although this kind of reasoning is not limited to making generalizations about people, i.e. from the sample of participants in the experiment to a populaton which they represent, it is this aspect which is most common and which illustrates the principle most clearly.

Suppose we are interested in carrying out experiments with children between eight and ten years old. Because virtually all children of these ages attend school it is not too difficult, given the necessary permissions, to obtain a list of such children within a particular Local Education Authority. This set of children might constitute the population for your studies. Note that unless you have a way of tracking down children not on the schools' books – e.g. those educated at home, or in private education outside the area, etc. – the population you are dealing with changes from all the children in the area to all those attending schools in the area. Even then there are grey areas; do you include all schools – opted out, private and special?

For a particular experiment you would select a representative sample of, say, sixty children from this population. Probably the best, and in principle (though not in practice) simplest way of doing this is through selection of a **random sample**. That means using some scheme which guarantees that each child in the population has an equal chance of appearing in the sample. Appendix 1 shows how this could be done. Such random sampling permits the generalizing of any findings about the sample tested to the population from which they are drawn and is central to much of the statistical reasoning developed later in the book.

It must be admitted, however, that in practice the use of random sampling from a known population to establish a set of participants is quite rare. Student experiments are commonly carried out on an incestuous basis where members of the class participate in each other's experiments or manage to persuade or cajole other students to take part. As the main purpose here is for the experimenter to develop skills and understanding in carrying out experiments, this shortcoming may not be too serious. Even in research carried out primarily to extend knowledge it is not unusual to depend on similar 'convenience' samples using whoever can be persuaded to take part. Does this matter? In one sense yes, as such experimenters are almost certainly using statistical techniques based on assumptions about representative sampling. In other senses the answer is probably no: the experimenter is in fact much more interested in establishing possible causal relationships than worrying about the generalizability of results.

## Three basic designs or how do participants fit into the experiment?

Given that we have chosen our IV and DV and decided on the way in which they will be operationally defined in the experimental situation, some of the most important decisions remaining relate to the way in which participants are assigned to the different conditions.

These ways of assignment lead to three basic experimental designs. These are given a variety of labels but will be referred to here as the **independent samples design**, the **matched pairs design** and the **repeated measures design**.

### 1 The independent samples design

For this design a group of participants is obtained for the experiment as a whole, and then individuals are allocated randomly to one or other of the experimental conditions. The term 'independent samples' arises from this randomness of allocation. If we decide to use sixteen participants in all, they will be allocated randomly to the two conditions. It is usual to do this allocation with the further stipulation or constraint that there are equal numbers in the two groups. This could be done using a coin with heads for condition A say, and tails for condition B, or, alternatively, using odds and evens from random number tables. We would continue allocating in this way until eight participants had been allocated to one of the two groups, when the remaining participants would be allocated to the other group.

The allocation might be as follows:

*Table 1* Allocation of participants in independent samples design

| condition A | condition B |
|---|---|
| $P_1$ | $P_3$ |
| $P_2$ | $P_6$ |
| $P_4$ | $P_7$ |
| $P_5$ | $P_8$ |
| $P_9$ | $P_{10}$ |
| $P_{12}$ | $P_{11}$ |
| $P_{13}$ | $P_{15}$ |
| $P_{14}$ | $P_{16}$ |

Here $P_1$ stands for participant one, $P_2$ for participant two, etc.

In the experiment each participant provides a single score for purposes of analysis, i.e. the total number of participants is the same as the total number of scores.

## 2 The matched pairs design

In this design, participants are matched in pairs and the two members of each pair allocated randomly, one to each of the experimental conditions. Any experimenter having access to pairs of identical twins would be addicted to this design, but there are other ways in which pairs can be obtained. The matching can be performed in terms of a third variable for which the experimenter has good evidence that it is likely to affect scores on the dependent variable. Thus in a problem-solving task, it would be possible to match participants in terms of intelligence. If IQ test scores are available, pairs of participants could be selected who were closely equated in terms of their measured IQs. In the 'absent-mindedness' experiment it might, for instance, have been feasible to match participants in terms of their performance on some appropriate memory task.

The allocation might be as shown in Table 2. Here $P_{11}$ stands for participant 1 in the first matched pair and $P_{12}$ stands for participant 2 in the first matched pair. $P_{21}$ stands for participant 1

*Table 2* Allocation of participants in matched pairs design

| condition A | condition B |
|---|---|
| $P_{12}$ | $P_{11}$ |
| $P_{21}$ | $P_{22}$ |
| $P_{31}$ | $P_{32}$ |
| $P_{42}$ | $P_{41}$ |
| $P_{51}$ | $P_{52}$ |
| $P_{62}$ | $P_{61}$ |
| $P_{71}$ | $P_{72}$ |
| $P_{82}$ | $P_{81}$ |

in the second matched pair, and so on. The decision about whether participant 1 or participant 2 within each pair is allocated to condition A or to condition B is on a random basis. As with the independent samples design, each participant provides a single score for analysis, the total number of participants again being the same as the total number of scores.

## 3 The repeated measures design

In this design, a single participant appears under both of the experimental conditions. Thus for the same number of scores as the other two designs we only need half the number of participants.

*Table 3* Allocation of participants in repeated measures design

| condition A | condition B |
|---|---|
| $P_1$ | $P_1$ |
| $P_2$ | $P_2$ |
| $P_3$ | $P_3$ |
| $P_4$ | $P_4$ |
| $P_5$ | $P_5$ |
| $P_6$ | $P_6$ |
| $P_7$ | $P_7$ |
| $P_8$ | $P_8$ |

Here $P_1$ stands for the same participant under both experimental conditions, $P_2$ stands for a second participant, who also appears under both conditions, and so on.

Although there are obviously no problems here in terms of the allocation of participants to the different experimental conditions there are special problems relating to the *order* in which each participant performs the two experimental conditions.

## Order effects in repeated measures designs

The change in the DV produced by the change in IV is called an **experimental effect**. However, as we have previously discussed, there may well be changes in the DV produced by variables other than the IV – unless we are able to control the effects of these other variables. In a repeated measures design there may be some systematic effect associated with the order in which a participant is involved with the two conditions; i.e. an **order effect**. Thus it might be that in a particular situation there is a general practice effect (increased familiarity with the situation, 'learning how to learn', etc.) such that whatever is done second tends to get a higher score irrespective of any effect of the IV. Alternatively, it might be that there is a negative practice effect of a general kind (fatigue, boredom, etc.) such that whatever is done second tends to get the lower score.

In either case we cannot make unambiguous statements about the experimental effect, i.e. as to whether condition A or condition B produces the better results, because what we actually measure is the combination of the experimental effect and the order effect. Clearly, if each participant were to be tested with condition A first and then condition B afterwards the experimental effect is inextricably mixed up with any order effect (this is referred to as the effects of the two variables being **confounded**). Two methods are commonly used to try to sort this out.

## Counterbalancing

In using counterbalancing some scheme is used so that half of the participants work under condition A first, and half work under condition B first. A simple version of this is shown in Table 4. Counterbalancing will only balance out an order effect in certain

*Table 4* Counterbalancing participants

| condition A | condition B |
| --- | --- |
| $P_1$ (first) | $P_1$ (second) |
| $P_2$ (second) | $P_2$ (first) |
| $P_3$ (first) | $P_3$ (second) |
| $P_4$ (second) | $P_4$ (first) |
| $P_5$ (first) | $P_5$ (second) |
| $P_6$ (second) | $P_6$ (first) |
| $P_7$ (first) | $P_7$ (second) |
| $P_8$ (second) | $P_8$ (first) |

circumstances. It would, for example, do this where the order effect is adding a constant amount to the score of whatever comes second. Unfortunately, it is quite possible that the order effect is more complicated. There could be a large order effect when condition A comes first, and only a small order effect when condition B comes first. This kind of effect is called an **interaction** and if it occurs, counterbalancing will only partially balance out the order effect. The basic problem, however, is that we usually do not know the nature of any possible order effect and hence can't be sure that it has been adequately dealt with.

## Randomization

An alternative to counterbalancing is randomization. This means we could decide by some random process, such as tossing a coin separately for each participant, whether he or she does condition A or condition B first. A fuller discussion of randomization and its relation to statistical inference follows in the next chapter. There are suggestions for methods of randomization in different situations in Appendix 1 (p. 149).

## Individual versus group designs

The three basic designs discussed in the preceding section are all group designs. A group of participants are selected and, after their involvement in the experiment, comparisons are made between group scores on the dependent variable under the two experimental conditions. However, while in some areas of psychology (such as aspects of social psychology) we are interested in group behaviour in its own right, it is more usually the case that what we are really interested in is individual behaviour.

Why use groups then? The main reason is that humans are complex and even in well controlled experiments there is likely to be considerable variability in their response. Often so much so that it is very difficult to discern any effects of the independent variable in the face of what amounts to a large amount of random variability of individual response. Using both groups and statistical analysis helps in sorting this out. But it is at the expense of finding things out about the average participant, rather than any one individual.

There is an influential approach within experimental psychology pioneered by B. F. Skinner which rejects such group designs. It depends on demonstrating effects within the individual subject as changes from a steady 'baseline'. Skinner argues that, using his techniques, it should be possible to exert such a degree of control over extraneous variables that the effect of changes in the independent variable becomes so clear and obvious that statistical analysis is unnecessary. A clear exposition of this alternative methodology is given in Sidman (1960). It is particularly influential in some areas of applied psychology, for example in behaviour modification studies carried out by clinical or educational psychologists.

Figure 1 illustrates an example. The first step in this type of study is to establish a **baseline**. This is a steady state of responding over several periods or sessions which must be established prior to any intervention by the experimenter. When this has been achieved, the experimenter changes the experimental conditions and measures responding over a further set of sessions. In a simple version of this kind of design, the experimenter then returns to the initial baseline condition and again measures responding for several sessions.

The results shown in Figure 1 provide a convincing demonstration of the effect of the IV on the DV (rate of responding) because there is a substantial and stable change from a stable baseline, to which responding returns after the intervention. You might reasonably ask: what does one do if the picture is not as clear-cut as this?

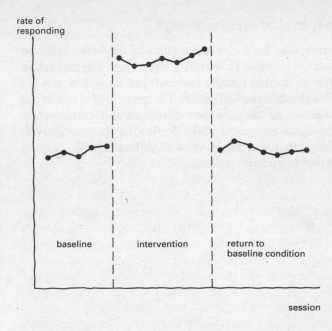

rate of
responding

baseline | intervention | return to
baseline condition

session

Figure 1   Example of simple baseline design

In this situation, Skinner puts the onus on you as experimenter to do a better experiment. You may need to control other variables more effectively so that the baseline becomes stable. Or slightly modify the intervention so that its effect becomes more clear-cut. Basically, the effects of the IV should be so unambiguous that you can simply 'eyeball' the data without need for statistical analysis.

This simple design (sometimes called an ABA design – referring to the baseline/intervention/and return to baseline phases respectively – has its problems. If used in an applied setting, where the intervention is usually seeking to bring about some desired change or improvement in behaviour, it is unfortunate and possibly unethical that the participant ends up where he or she started! So-called multiple-baseline designs and other more complex designs avoid such problems.

## Are you ready to start experimenting?

No. The discussion so far has covered some of the issues involved in designing an experiment. However, a basic rule of experimentation is that *you do not start unless and until you know how you are going to analyse the data you will obtain.* The next chapter provides a general introduction to the principles of statistical inference which underlie the analyses you might make. Following chapters provide a range of things that you might do with different kinds of data. Chapter 8 returns to matters of design.

# 3   Statistical inference

## Constant and random error

In a simple experiment, we are trying to find the effect, if any, that the independent variable has on the dependent variable. As discussed in the last chapter, the dependent variable may be affected by variables other than the independent variable. We concentrated there on variables producing an order effect, but there is a whole host of other variables which might affect the dependent variable. Such variables can be thought of as producing two kinds of errors when we are trying to work out the effect of the independent variable – **random errors** and **constant errors**.

For example, in experiments with animals, food is often used as a reward for food-deprived animals. The method commonly used at one time to ensure that they were appropriately food-deprived was to allow access to food for only a short time, say thirty minutes, per day. However, different animals would take in different amounts of food during this time. If performance in some task were related to food deprivation, then there would be variations in performance which would contribute unpredictable errors, likely to be random in their effect, to any experiment using this method of food deprivation.

A constant error would occur if, for some reason, all the animals in one experimental condition were able to eat for longer than those in another condition. Hence the direction of the error would always be the same and constant in its effect.

Notice that random and constant errors have different effects: **a random error obscures** the experimental effect we are interested in, **a constant error biases** or distorts the results.

## Constant errors must go!

Our business in designing an experiment is to hunt down all possible sources of constant error. In some cases it is possible to eliminate them completely by means of *direct control*. To take a fanciful but hopefully clear example: a constant error would be introduced in comparing heights of eskimo and pygmy children if a ruler were used which expanded as the temperature increased (assuming pygmies live in warmer climates than eskimos!). This could be controlled and completely eliminated by using a non-expanding ruler. Less fancifully, if we are carrying out an experiment where there are likely to be gender differences in performance which are not in themselves the focus of our interest then we could use direct control by working solely with females (or solely with males). In other cases one may not be able to control directly, but the biasing effect can be removed either by counterbalancing (as in the case of simple order effects) or, more generally, by randomization. However, neither counter-balancing nor randomization eliminates the error. They merely have the effect of transforming it from constant error to random error. This means that they remove the error as a source of bias, but it still remains to obscure the experimental effect in which we are interested. Whilst it may appear desirable to eliminate all possible constant errors by direct control, there are arguments against this.

Consider what might be called the 'left-handed, fifty-three-year-old introverted Isle of Wight rat-catcher' approach to experimentation. In setting up a particular hypothetical experiment it might appear likely that the handedness of the subjects would be related to their performance. Using direct control we would decide to work either entirely with left-handers, or entirely with right-handers – say the former. Similarly, age could be seen as a possible variable, and using direct control we would opt for a particular age or age range for our subjects. In like manner, personality variables, geographical location and profession might also be seen as having a potential effect in our experiment. Clearly the end result is ludicrous. It is highly unlikely that we would be able to find even a single individual to fit the bill, let alone a viable group to carry out the experiment. And even if by some miracle this were possible, the generality of any results we obtained would be highly questionable.

Put in more general terms it may well be that the effects of an IV on a DV can be demonstrated when everything within sight is held constant. However, it may possibly happen that this effect is dependent on the particular values of one or more of the variables held constant. If we had held them constant at a different value, then the experimental effect might have disappeared.

The main alternative to direct control is randomization, i.e. we allow things to vary but seek to ensure their random allocation to the different conditons of the experiment. If the experimental effect still stands when these variables have been randomized, it indicates that the effect is reasonably robust.

## Random errors will not go!

Some random errors can be eliminated as, for example, those caused by the animals eating different amounts during their thirty-minute feeding period. A better method, now widely used, is to feed the animals a carefully measured amount of food which maintains them at a given percentage of their free-feeding body weight. Thus if we can assume that the effect of food deprivation is directly dependent on this percentage, the random error attributable to differences in food deprivation can be completely eliminated.

However, there are many random errors which cannot be eliminated in this way. Consider the many things which might affect a human participant's performance on a memory or a learning task. In order to control these effects one would need a set of participants with identical heredity and environment. Their learning and other experiences before the experiment would have to be equated. They would need to be of the same intelligence and have the same personality and attitudes, to be in the same state of health, etc., etc. The list is endless and it would be impossible to contemplate even starting any experiments if this kind of control were a necessary prerequisite. One is forced to conclude that random error is here to stay and that our methods will have to take this into account.

To this end, the basic strategy is to make sure that the allocation of participants to the different experimental conditions is random so that any potential constant errors end up as random errors.

## Statistical inference and probability

Granted, then, that random error will be present, both in its own right and as a result of our having randomized constant errors, how can it be disentangled from the experimental effect that we are after? The answer is that we make use of **statistical inference**.

What we do is:

1 *Estimate how probable it is that the random error by itself could produce the changes in the dependent variable observed in the experiment.*

If

2 *It seems unlikely that random error by itself could produce these changes*

then

3 *We decide that it is the independent variable which is having an effect on the dependent variable.*

You should work through this argument several times. The idea is very important and the process is the reverse of what many people expect. Instead of coming to a decision about the independent variable's effect directly, we approach it indirectly by discounting the likelihood that the effect was produced by random error.

Statistics is used to make inferences about these effects – hence the term 'statistical inference'. Before we can do this you need to have some understanding of the concept of 'probability'.

## Probability

The concept of probability is controversial among both statisticians and philosophers. It is used in at least three different ways. In everyday life the reference is usually to how likely or unlikely it is that a future event will occur. Thus we have statements such as 'Huddersfield Town will probably win on Saturday' or 'You'll probably be sick if you eat that third cream cake'. Sometimes this feeling of doubt or uncertainty is expressed in numerical terms as 'I think it's 10 to 1 against him stopping smoking in the New Year' but even so these are subjective estimates and as such this use of the term is commonly referred to as **subjective probability**.

A second use of the term derives from analyses of card games and other games of chance. In cutting a well-shuffled pack of playing cards what is the probability that the card turned over is an ace? This approach defines **probability as the ratio of the number of favourable cases** (here the four aces) **to the total number of equally likely cases** (here the fifty-two cards, assuming a normal pack with no jokers). The probability is then 1 in 13, otherwise expressed as 1/13. This idea, particularly the notion of 'equally likely cases', enables one to work out theoretically the probability of various events occurring in quite complex situations and is of considerable value to casino owners and the like. You should note, however, that this is a formal, theoretical approach to probability sometimes referred to as **mathematical probability**, and the extent to which it corresponds to real life in any situation depends on whether the theoretical assumptions (and particularly the idea of equally likely cases) apply in that actual situation. When playing with dice it seems reasonable to assume that each of the six alternatives resulting from rolling a single die is equally likely. However, such things as loaded dice are not unknown and if over a period we find in practice that, say, a 1 comes up in over half the rolls, then the applicability of the theory in this case is cast into considerable doubt.

This last example illustrates a third approach to probability, the so-called 'relative frequency' approach, otherwise known as **empirical probability**. Here the probability of an event is estimated by the ratio of the number of times the event occurs to the total number of trials which have taken place. It is an estimate because the actual number of trials which have taken place are regarded as a sample from the almost infinitely large population of trials which could theoretically take place. The probability is the state of affairs in this population and will tend to be more and more accurately estimated as we increase the size of the sample. Anyone with a few days to spare might like to test this by tossing a coin repeatedly and noting the proportion of heads obtained after, say, ten trials, a hundred trials, a thousand trials, etc.

These three approaches to probability are not necessarily incompatible. In particular the mathematical and empirical approach often helpfully complement each other. The mathematical approach to coin tossing obviously gives a probability of a half for heads and various lengthy series of coin tosses which have been carried out give estimates, as one might expect subjectively, that are essentially the same (although some types of coin give a very small but consistent 'heads' bias, presumably because of a slight asymmetry in the coin itself).

Probability (given the symbol $p$) is commonly expressed numerically with a minimum value of 0 and a maximum value of 1: 0 refers to something which never occurs and 1 to something which always occurs. In practice, of course, most of the things in which we are interested are somewhere between these extremes and hence have values larger than 0 and smaller than 1.

Consider an experiment. Suppose that in a design where we have pairs of scores (either the matched pairs or repeated measures design) we found that in seven out of eight pairs, scores are larger in condition A than in condition B. And that in only one out of eight pairs the score was higher in condition B than in condition A. (We are going to assume, to make things simpler, that it is not possible to get a tie.) What is the probability that we would have obtained that result on a chance basis, i.e. if only random effects are involved and there is no effect due to the experimental conditions (i.e. no effect of the IV on the DV)?

To simplify the explanation let us refer to the pair where condition A scores are higher than condition B as a '+'; and the pair where they score lower as a '−'. Using mathematical probability we can take the assumption that only random effects are involved as equivalent to the assumption of equally likely outcomes. That is, the probability of getting a + with any pair is $\frac{1}{2}$ (a half), and the probability of getting a − is also $\frac{1}{2}$. If you find it easier, think in terms of the probability of getting 'heads' when you toss a coin.

Suppose we consider two pairs together. There are then three possibilities: two +s (i.e. both pairs A scores larger than B scores); one + (one pair A larger than B, the other B larger than A); and zero +s (both pairs B larger than A). What are the probabilities associated with these? A 'family tree' helps to demonstrate this (Figure 2).

There is a total of *four* possible outcomes. It is reasonable to assume that each of the four are equally likely. They are − first, pair 1 getting + and pair 2 getting +; second, pair 1 getting +

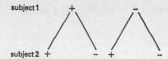

Figure 2 'Family tree' for two participants

and pair 2 getting $-$; third, pair 1 getting $-$ and pair 2 getting $+$; fourth, pair 1 getting $-$ and pair 2 getting $-$. Considering these four possible outcomes, two $+$s occurs once in four (i.e. $p = \frac{1}{4} = 0.25$), one $+$ occurs twice in four (i.e. $p = \frac{2}{4} = 0.5$) and zero $+$s occurs once in four (i.e. $p = \frac{1}{4} = 0.25$).

In this way it is possible to work out the probability, on a chance basis, of getting any given number of $+$s with any total number of pairs. For example, with four pairs, the 'family tree' looks like Figure 3.

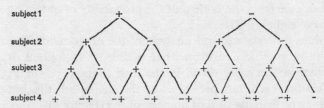

Figure 3 'Family tree' for four participants

There is a total of sixteen possible outcomes and a table of probabilities can be obtained as shown in Table 5.

*Table 5* Probabilities for different numbers of $+$s with four pairs

| Number of $+$s | Probability ( = fraction of outcomes) |
| --- | --- |
| 4 | $\frac{1}{16} = 0.0625$ |
| 3 | $\frac{4}{16} = 0.2500$ |
| 2 | $\frac{6}{16} = 0.3750$ |
| 1 | $\frac{4}{16} = 0.2500$ |
| 0 | $\frac{1}{16} = 0.0625$ |

Returning to our original example of eight pairs, the drawing of the family tree is left to the reader, the total number of possible

*Table 6* Probabilities for different numbers of +s with eight pairs

| Number of +s | Probability (= fraction of outcomes) |
|---|---|
| 8 | $\frac{1}{256} = 0.004$ |
| 7 | $\frac{8}{256} = 0.031$ |
| 6 | $\frac{28}{256} = 0.110$ |
| 5 | $\frac{56}{256} = 0.220$ |
| 4 | $\frac{70}{256} = 0.270$ |
| 3 | $\frac{56}{256} = 0.220$ |
| 2 | $\frac{28}{256} = 0.110$ |
| 1 | $\frac{8}{256} = 0.031$ |
| 0 | $\frac{1}{256} = 0.004$ |

outcomes now being 256. The table of probabilities is given in Table 6. We can see from the table that the probability of obtaining seven +s out of eight is 0.031.

But how does this relate to our analysis of the experiment? This can be shown in graphical form in what is called a histogram or bar chart (discussed in more detail in the next chapter, p. 40). A bar is drawn for each number of +s, the height of the bar representing the probability of that number of +s (Figure 4).

## Significance level

Recall that the decision is made that the independent variable has affected the dependent variable when the probability of getting the result obtained, if random errors only are involved, is sufficiently low.

The histogram shown in Figure 4 gives the distribution of the number of +s out of eight when it is pure chance whether or not any particular result ends up as + or −. Look at the extremes of this distribution. The probability of getting no +s at all is 0.004, i.e very low. Similarly the probability of getting all +s is 0.004. We might feel that these probabilities are so low that we are justified in deciding that results as extreme as this (i.e. all of the eight going in the same direction) are not due to random errors alone. If they are not due to the random errors, and we have got rid of the constant

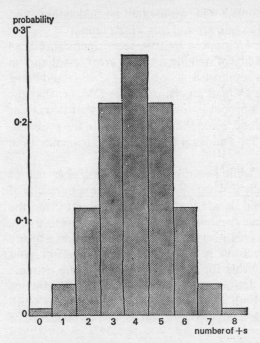

Figure 4   Histogram showing the probabilities for different number of +s with eight participants

errors, then this result must be due to the effect of the independent variable.

How low does the probability have to be for us to make this kind of decision? There is no definitive answer to the question. Whatever level we choose, it is possible to make an error. In fact, there are two possible kinds of error. What is usually called a **type 1 error** occurs when we decide that the independent variable had an effect on the dependent variable when it did not have an effect (i.e. when, in fact, the change in the dependent variable was due to the random effects alone). A **type 2 error** occurs when we conclude that the independent variable had no effect on the dependent variable when, in fact, there was a genuine relationship.

What is normally done is to choose a **significance level**. The significance level is simply the probability of making a type 1 error.

The meaning of significance level is quite often misunderstood, and it will perhaps be useful to talk around this a little more.

Refer back to Figure 4. Suppose that we set a significance level of $p < 0.01$ (i.e. probability of making a type 1 error less than 1 in a hundred) then, with a result of 8 +s or of 0 +s, we would come to the decision that the IV had an effect on the DV, i.e. that the result was sufficiently improbable for us to decide that it was not due to random errors alone. Note that this is because the probability of 8 +s and that of 0 +s adds up to 0.008 which is smaller than 0.01.

Suppose that we are willing to take a somewhat higher risk of making a type 1 error, say $p < 0.1$. You can see that with results of 8, 7, 1 or 0 +s we would decide that the IV had an effect on the DV. This is because their combined probability adds up to 0.070, which is smaller than 0.1. Notice here that, if you are going to say that with 7 +s the decision is that the IV has an effect, you obviously must also say this for 8 +s, i.e. for any more extreme result. Also that we are deciding this irrespective of the direction of the difference, i.e. that both a large proportion of +s and a small proportion of +s (hence a large proportion of −s) are evidence of an effect.

The lower the probability set for the significance level – and hence the less chance of making a type 1 error – the greater the chance of making a type 2 error. In other words, by limiting your decision that the IV affects the DV to the very extreme cases, you are making it more likely that in some cases you will decide incorrectly that there was no effect. So some kind of balance has to be struck between these two errors.

There is a convention whereby a significance level of probability $p < 0.05$ (the 5 per cent significance level) is referred to as **statistically significant** (sometimes simply referred to as **significant**). It must be stressed that this is simply a convention, an agreement between consenting experimentalists. There is nothing magic about the 5 per cent figure. It may be (for example, in exploratory research into an area) that one is worried about type 2 errors, i.e. about regarding as non-significant a relationship which perhaps ought to be followed up, and hence that a significance level of $p < 0.1$ might be preferable. On the other hand, there are situations

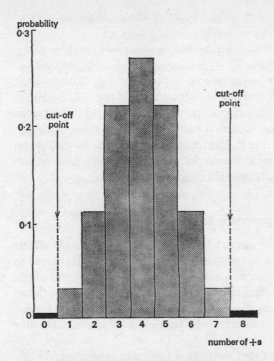

Figure 5    Histogram from Figure 4 with cut-off points added

where the consequences of making a type 1 error might be particularly worrying (owing, perhaps, to one's findings and conclusions being at variance with other published work), and a significance level of $p < 0.01$ or smaller might be indicated. Incidentally the $p < 0.01$ or 1 per cent significance level is sometimes referred to as **highly significant**.

If we decide, however, to be conventional and to use, say, a 5 per cent ($p < 0.05$) significance level, what decision do we come to in our experiment? Referring back to the histogram showing the distribution of +s (Figure 4), the significance level is used to divide the dependent variable into two regions – a region where we will decide that random effects alone are involved and one where we will decide that the independent variable did have an effect on the variable. A glance at Table 6 (p. 32) reveals that, if the cut-off points are marked as shown in Figure 5, the total probability of making a type 1 error is $p = 0.008$.

If the cut-off point had been moved in to include the 1 + and 7 + cases, the total probability of making a type 1 error increases to $p = 0.070$. This latter value would exceed the significance level, which we had set at $p < 0.05$ – i.e. too much of the distribution is being cut off and the cut-off points actually shown on the diagram should be used. As our observed number of +s in the experiment was 7, we see that this lies in the region 'decide IV had no effect on DV' and hence we cannot regard this as evidence for a relationship between independent variable and dependent variable.

## Hypotheses and hypothesis testing

You will often find that issues about whether or not the IV affects the DV are referred to in terms of the **null hypothesis** ($H_0$) and the **alternative hypothesis** ($H_1$). In this language, the null hypothesis is that the IV does not affect the DV. Various alternative hypotheses are possible, but the most general one would be that the IV does affect the DV (stated in terms of the particular IV and DV in your experiment).

When the experiment and analysis are completed we then

*either*    reject $H_0$ and accept $H_1$, if the result is less probable than the chosen significance level;

*or*    accept $H_0$ and reject $H_1$ if the result is equal to or more probable than the chosen significance level.

Some statisticians consider it inappropriate to talk about 'accepting' $H_0$ and prefer 'fail to reject' $H_0$ instead. This is because in 'accepting' $H_0$ we don't mean that it is likely that $H_0$ is true, only that we don't have evidence to reject it.

## A warning about the (lack of) significance of statistical significance

There is some tendency for experimenters to worship statistical significance. This is in part because it is much easier to secure publication for a 'significant' finding than for one which is 'non-significant'. In some ways this is very understandable. The discovery of causal relationships between variables is central to much science. Also, poorly performed and controlled experiments are likely to produce non-significant findings.

The difficulty with the concept is that there is a tendency to jump from 'statistical significance' to 'significance' in the sense of 'importance'. All that statistical significance tells you is that what you have found is unlikely to be explicable in terms of random errors. Given a well-designed experiment you can make the leap to saying that it is likely that the IV has had a causal effect on the DV. It says nothing about the size or importance of the effect. In fact, an almost sure-fire way of achieving statistical significance is simply to increase the size of the sample taking part in your experiment. Larger samples provide a more sensitive test of differences between the experimental conditions and there will almost inevitably be some kind of effect which is detectable with a sufficiently large sample. So while it is tempting, and true, to say that your non-significant result in an experiment may point to the need for a larger-scale study, it is actually the significant results from well-designed relatively small-scale studies that are going to pick up the more important 'robust' experimental findings.

## The sign test

It is perfectly possible to work out the probabilities of different outcomes for any number of pluses and minuses, through the 'family tree' method. This does, however, become somewhat laborious – particularly for large samples. The **sign test** provides a simple way of reaching the same conclusions. It involves looking up the number of pluses (or the number of minuses; whichever is the smaller) against the total number of pluses and minuses in a table. The table then tells you whether the result you have obtained is statistically significant at the 5 per cent level.

A step-by-step procedure and worked example for doing this are given overleaf on pp. 38 and 39.

## Step-by-step procedure

### Sign test

Use this test when you have pairs of scores (i.e. matched pairs or repeated measures designs)

**Step 1** Give each pair of scores a plus ($+$) if the score in the left-hand condition exceeds that in the right-hand condition, a minus ($-$) if the score in the left-hand condition is less than that in the right-hand condition, a zero (0) if there is no difference.

**Step 2** Note the number of times ($L$) the less frequent sign occurs and the total number ($T$) of pluses and minuses. *Ignore all zeros*, i.e. do not include them in $T$.

**Step 3** Look up in Table B (p. 161) the highest value of $L$ which is significant at the 5% level for this value of $T$.

**Step 4** If your value of $L$ is equal to or lower than the value obtained from the table, the decision is made that the IV had an effect on the DV – the results are referred to as 'significant at the 5% level'. If your value of $L$ is greater than the table value, then the decision is made that the independent variable had no effect on the dependent variable – the results are 'not significant'.

**Step 5** Translate the result of the statistical test back in terms of the experiment.

## Worked example

### Sign test

The following scores were obtained in a matched pairs design with nine pairs of participants.

| A | B | Step 1 |
|----|----|--------|
| 12 | 7 | + |
| 10 | 8 | + |
| 15 | 11 | + |
| 8 | 8 | 0 |
| 7 | 8 | – |
| 10 | 9 | + |
| 8 | 4 | + |
| 7 | 5 | + |
| 13 | 9 | + |

**Step 2** $L = 1$, $T = 8$

**Step 3** From Table B, highest value of $L = 0$ for significance when $T = 8$.

**Step 4** As our value of $L$ is greater than this we decide that the IV has no effect on the DV – i.e. the results are not significant.

**Step 5** The difference between condition A and condition B is not significant at the 5% level.

*Note* (a) The results obtained are identical to those obtained by a direct calculation of probabilities (p. 36).

(b) Although the results are not significant, there is a suggestion that there are higher scores under condition A; this should perhaps be explored in a more extensive experiment (or with a more sensitive test).

# 4 Descriptive statistics

## What are descriptive statistics?

Even a quite small experiment can generate large amounts of data; columns of times, or numbers of errors, or some other scores. It can then be difficult to see what has been going on. This calls for ways in which you can summarize the data. Descriptive statistics do this – they are, in fact, sometimes referred to as 'summary statistics'.

This chapter concentrates on two aspects of a set of data which are commonly summarized. These are covered by statistics which describe the **most typical value** (some kind of **average**); and how much **variability** there is about this central value. There is then discussion of a third statistic which describes the relationship between two sets of data (known as **correlation**).

While these descriptive statistics are extremely useful, do not neglect the opportunities that graphs of various kinds present in displaying and summarizing data. We already came across this in the previous chapter where the **histogram** of Figure 4 provides a much more vivid representation of the probabilities of different numbers of +s than does Table 6. It is worth noting that, when displaying a variable in the form of categories (e.g. 'female' and 'male'; or different ethnic origins) it is the convention to show these as separate, non-touching bars as in Figure 6.

Such graphs (sometimes referred to as **bar charts** or **bar graphs**) emphasize that there are no intermediate values and that the ordering along the axis (males on the left or right) is arbitrary.

For similar reasons the use of standard **line graphs** should be restricted to situations where the variable along the horizontal axis

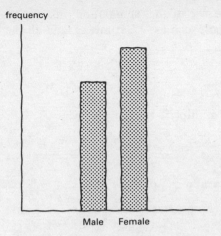

frequency

Male    Female

Figure 6   Histogram (bar chart) with categorical variables

is continuous (e.g. age or height). Only then are intermediate values between the points on the graph meaningful.

## Measures of central tendency

### 1 The mean

This is a very commonly used measure of *most typical value*. You probably already know it as the average, obtained by adding all the scores together and then dividing by the number of scores.

It can be used to provide an introduction to some of the symbols widely used in statistics. Scores in general are commonly represented by the symbol $X$; the first score by $X_1$; the second by $X_2$ and so on. If there is a total of $N$ scores, then the last of these is represented by $X_N$. The mean itself is given a special symbol $\bar{X}$, usually referred to as '$X$ bar'.

$$\bar{X} = \frac{\text{total of all scores}}{\text{total number of scores}} = \frac{X_1 + X_2 + X_3 + \ldots + X_N}{N}.$$

This can be simplified by the use of the 'summation' instruction 'Σ'. Placed in front of a symbol, such as '$X$', it means 'add all the $X$s together'.

$$\bar{X} = \frac{\Sigma X}{N}$$

(Note that $\Sigma X$ does *not* mean 'multiply $\Sigma$ by $X$'.)

For example, if the scores are

7, 3, 11, 12, 9, 14

then   $\Sigma X = 7 + 3 + 11 + 12 + 9 + 14 = 56$

and   $N = 6$

so

$$\bar{X} = \frac{\Sigma X}{N} = \frac{56}{6} = 9{\cdot}3,$$

i.e. the mean is 9·3.

Strictly speaking, the proper label for an average calculated in this way is the 'arithmetic mean'. This is to distinguish it from other kinds of mean (the 'geometric' and 'harmonic' means) which are used for special purposes. However, the arithmetic mean is much more commonly used and will be the one assumed if you simply refer to the 'mean'.

## 2 The median

The median is the central value in a set of scores. It is obtained by arranging the scores in order of size. With an odd number of scores the median is simply the score which then has equal numbers of scores above and below it. With an even number of scores, it is the average of the two central scores. (There are more complicated formulae for calculating the median with an even number of scores, but the result seldom differs appreciably from simply taking the average of the two central scores.) If there is a cluster of scores around the centre, all having the same value, then the simplest procedure is to regard that value as being the median.

As an example, if the scores are:

14, 9, 17, 21, 7, 18, 16, 22

then, rearranging these scores in increasing order of size we get:

7, 9, 14, 16, 17, 18, 21, 22.

As there are eight scores, the median is the average of the fourth and fifth scores:

$$\frac{16 + 17}{2} = 16{\cdot}5$$

i.e. the median is 16·5.

## 3 The mode

The mode is the value which occurs most frequently in a set of scores. It usually only makes sense to use the mode as a measure of central tendency when you have a large set of scores. Even then it may be necessary to group scores together (i.e. to put together all scores in a certain range, say from 21 to 25 cms, 26 to 30 cms, etc.).

If a histogram is plotted, the highest frequency is given by the longest bar in the histogram and hence gives you the mode. Figure 7 shows an example where grouping has taken place. When dealing with scores which are ordered in this way, it is possible for there to be a second major peak in the distribution of scores displayed in a histogram. This is called a **bimodal** distribution and is best dealt with by displaying the histogram rather than by quoting the mode.

## Mean, median and mode compared

The mean is the statistic most commonly used as a measure of central tendency. One reason for this is its sensitivity; in the sense that if any one of the scores in a set of scores changes, then the mean will change. In contrast, both the median and the mode may well be unaffected by changing the value of several scores. Try this out for yourself.

While this sensitivity is often an advantage it can be a disadvantage. Suppose the following scores represent times in seconds to solve some anagrams:

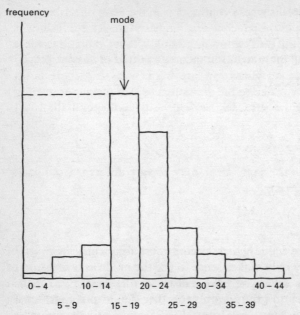

Figure 7 Mode derived from histogram

1, 2, 2, 3, 4, 5, 5, 6, 224

the mean works out at 28. However, this mean is a very strange 'most typical value'. What we have in the set of scores is a quite tightly clustered group well below ten seconds, and a 'rogue' score (the technical term for this is an **outlier**) where, perhaps, the person involved had some kind of block in solving the anagram. 28 seconds is not typical of either. Here, the median (4 seconds) would be the most appropriate central tendency statistic to use, simply because it is insensitive to the values of extreme scores.

Note that the median (and the mode) can still be calculated when some extreme values are unknown; say when a participant has such a block that they find an anagram impossible to solve and all you can record is 'over 5 minutes'.

There are some kinds of data where it is not possible to calculate a mean. An example is where your data is in the form of rankings or orderings (i.e. you know which is first, highest, longest, etc.; which is second and so on, but don't know any actual scores). It is still feasible to work out a median though. If you have the kind of data displayed in Figure 7, where all you know are frequencies and there is no appropriate way of ordering the data, then neither mean nor median is feasible and you are left with the mode as the only possibility.

## Measures of dispersion

Sets of scores with the same mean may be very different from each other. Consider the set:

17, 32, 34, 58, 69, 70, 98, 142

and a second set of:

61, 62, 64, 65, 65, 66, 68, 69.

Both have means of 65, but the **dispersion** (otherwise known as **variability** or **spread**) of the second set is much smaller than that of the first set. Several statistics have been devised to measure this aspect of a set of data.

## 1 Range

The range is the difference between the highest and lowest scores. It is, therefore, very easy to compute. As an example, take the following scores arranged in order of size:

19, 21, 22, 22, 25, 27, 28, 42.

The range is highest minus lowest,

i.e. **range** $= 42 - 19 = 23$.

The main disadvantage of the range as a measure of dispersion is that it is just based on these two extreme scores. Such scores may be suspect and it may be unwise to give them undue weight. For example, an abnormally long time to respond in some task may be due to the participant day-dreaming or otherwise not attending rather than to the difficulty of the task.

## 2 Semi-interquartile range

This is a more sophisticated type of range statistic. If the scores are arranged in ascending order of size, the point that cuts off the lowest quarter of the scores is called the **first quartile** $(Q_1)$. The point that cuts off the lowest three quarters of the scores is called the **third quartile** $(Q_3)$. If, for instance, there are 24 scores, the first quartile $(Q_1)$ occurs between the 6th and 7th scores (take the average of 6th and 7th scores, as for the median). The third quartile $(Q_3)$ occurs between the 18th and 19th scores (again, take their average).

The interquartile range is the difference between the third and first quartiles. As the name suggests, the semi-interquartile range is half of this,

i.e. **semi-interquartile range** $= \dfrac{Q_3 - Q_1}{2}$.

This measure of range is commonly used when the median is used as a measure of central tendency. (Note that the median, the central point in a set of scores, has half of the scores below it and can also be referred to as the **second quartile**.)

The relative sizes of the differences $(Q_3 - Q_2)$ and $(Q_2 - Q_1)$ provides a useful measure of the **skewness** (or lack of symmetry) of the distribution of a set of scores. Figure 8 shows three histograms. One has a longer 'tail' to the left (lower scores) than to the right (higher scores). This is called a **negative skew**. A second one is symmetrical. The third has a longer tail to the right (higher scores) than to the left (lower scores). This is called a **positive skew**.

In terms of the quartiles:

There is a negative skew if $(Q_2 - Q_1) > (Q_3 - Q_2)$,
and positive skew if $(Q_2 - Q_1) < (Q_3 - Q_2)$.

The advantage of the semi-interquartile range over the range as a measure of dispersion is that it is not simply dependent on the two extreme values.

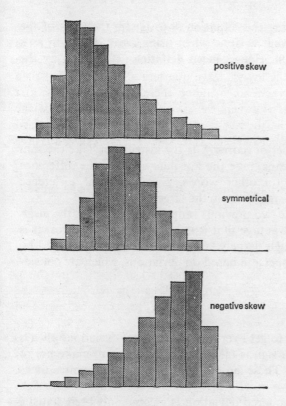

Figure 8 Positive and negative skew

## 3  Mean deviation

The **deviation** $(x)$ of a score is the difference of that score from the mean. In symbols, if $X$ is a score, and $\bar{X}$ the mean score, then the deviation $x$ is given by

$$x = X - \bar{X}.$$

On first thoughts, it might appear very sensible to use the average of such deviations as a measure of dispersion. However, if you do this, taking note of the fact that some deviations will be positive

47

and some negative, you will find that the average always comes out at zero! (Try it.)

One way of rescuing this situation is to ignore the signs of the deviations. This is what is done when using mean deviation as a measure of dispersion. Hence, **mean deviation** $(\bar{x})$ is given by the formula

$$\bar{x} = \frac{\Sigma|X - \bar{X}|}{N}$$

where $N$ is the number of scores; $\Sigma$ is the instruction 'take the sum of'; and $|X - \bar{X}|$ means 'take the absolute value of the difference between $X$ and $\bar{X}$' (in other words, always call the difference positive, i.e. take the smaller from the larger).

Compared with the two previous range-based statistics, the mean deviation has the advantage that it is based on all the scores. It is not widely used though, largely because it has been supplanted by other measures of dispersion based on deviations, which are considered below.

## 4 Variance

An alternative tactic to get over the problem that deviations always add up to zero when sign is taken into account, is to make use of squared deviations. These are always positive (as 'minus times minus is plus').

The mean of the squared deviation is a commonly used statistic and is called the **variance**. From our previous discussions you would expect the formula for variance to be

$$\text{Variance} = \frac{\Sigma(X - \bar{X})^2}{N}$$

where $X$ is the individual score
$\bar{X}$ is the mean score
$X - \bar{X}$ is the deviation
$(X - \bar{X})^2$ is the squared deviation
$\Sigma$ is the instruction 'take the sum of'
hence $\Sigma(X - \bar{X})^2$ means 'take the sum of the squared deviations'

and $N$ is the total number of scores.

This formula does give the variance of the actual set of scores you have in front of you. This is appropriate when you have a sample of scores and simply wish to describe various aspects of that sample. Or if you have measures from the whole of a population of some kind.

However, as has been stressed previously, the situation is more usually that we have a sample and want to make estimates about the state of affairs in the population from which the sample has been drawn. In these circumstances it can be shown (magic words!) that an unbiased estimate of the variance in the population is obtained by use of a slightly different formula:

$$\text{Variance} = \frac{\Sigma(X - \bar{X})^2}{N - 1}.$$

The $N - 1$ in the formula, which is substituted for the $N$ in the previous formula, is referred to as the **degrees of freedom**. As the name suggests it is the number of deviations from the mean which are free to vary. This is one less than $N$ because the final deviation is fixed by the need for the overall average deviation to be zero. This is by no means an adequate explanation for the use of $N - 1$ in the formula, but there is at least an intuitive rightness to the notion that our estimate of dispersion or variability should be divided by the number of things free to vary.

The effect of this change to the formula is to increase the estimate of variance. However, this makes little difference unless very small samples are used.

## 5 Standard deviation

A disadvantage of the variance as a measure of dispersion is that it is in squared units as compared with the original data (e.g. seconds squared rather than seconds). A simple solution to this is to take the square root of the variance. This is known as the **standard deviation (SD)**:

$$\text{SD} = \sqrt{\frac{\Sigma(X - \bar{X})^2}{N - 1}}.$$

This is by far the most commonly used of the measures of dispersion and would usually be paired with the mean as a measure of central tendency. Its popularity also arises from its links to the 'normal' distribution and various statistics associated with this distribution, as discussed in the next chapter.

If you are using a calculator (and we are now getting to statistics where it can be a substantial chore to do things by hand) a different version of the formula is marginally easier to deal with. This is

$$SD = \sqrt{\frac{\Sigma X^2 - (\Sigma X)^2/N}{N - 1}}$$

where $X$ is the individual score

$X^2$ is the individual score squared

$\Sigma X^2$ is the sum of the individual scores squared

$\Sigma X$ is the sum of the individual scores

$(\Sigma X)^2$ is the square of the sum of the individual scores

and $N$ is the total number of scores.

This formula can be derived by algebra from the previous one and hence leads to exactly the same result (assuming no arithmetical errors). You might like to check this using a small set of scores.

Just a word of warning. Take especial care not to confuse $\Sigma X^2$ – where you first square the scores and then add those squares together; and $(\Sigma X)^2$ – where you first add all the scores and then square the total.

## Step-by-step procedure

### Standard deviation

| *What to calculate* | *How to calculate it* | *Usual symbols* |
|---|---|---|
| **Step 1 total** | Add all the observations together | $\Sigma X$ |
| **Step 2 mean** | Divide the result of **step 1** by the number of observations | $\dfrac{\Sigma X}{N} = \bar{X}$ |
| **Step 3 uncorrected sum of squares** | (a) Square each of the observations<br>(b) Add all the squares together | $X^2$<br><br>$\Sigma X^2$ |
| **Step 4 correction term** | (a) Go back to the total obtained in **step 1** and square it<br>(b) Divide the result of **step 4a** by the number of observations | $(\Sigma X)^2$<br><br><br>$\dfrac{(\Sigma X)^2}{N}$ |
| **Step 5 corrected sum of squares** | Subtract the result of **step 4b** from that of **step 3b** | $\Sigma X^2 - \dfrac{(\Sigma X)^2}{N}$ |
| **Step 6 variance** | Divide the result of **step 5** by (number of observations $-$ 1) NB $(N - 1)$ is often referred to as 'degrees of freedom' | $\dfrac{\Sigma X^2 - (\Sigma X)^2/N}{(N - 1)}$ |
| **Step 7 standard deviation** | Take the square root of the result of **step 6** | $\sqrt{\dfrac{\Sigma X^2 - (\Sigma X)^2/N}{(N - 1)}}$ |

## Worked example

### Standard deviation

| Observations | | Step 3a $(Observations)^2$ |
|---|---|---|
| 4·5 | | 20·25 |
| 6·0 | | 36·00 |
| 7·4 | | 54·76 |
| 8·2 | | 67·24 |
| 2·1 | | 4·41 |
| 6·5 | | 42·25 |
| 5·4 | | 29·16 |
| ·9·3 | | 86·49 |
| 10·8 | | 116·64 |
| 8·0 | **Step 3b** | 64·00 |
| | **uncorrected** | |
| **Step 1 total** = 68·2 | **sum of squares** | 521·20 |

**Step 2 mean** $= \dfrac{68·2}{10} = 6·82$

**Step 4a** $= (68·2)^2$

**Step 4b**
**correction term** $= \dfrac{(68·2)^2}{10} = \dfrac{4651·2}{10} = 465·12$

**Step 5 corrected**
**sum of squares** $= 521·20 - 465·12 = 56·08$

**Step 6 variance** $= \dfrac{56·08}{9} = 6·23$

**Step 7 standard**
**variation** $= \sqrt{6·23} = 2·5$

## Standard scores

For purposes of comparison, say, of different individuals on the same test, or of the same person on different tests, it is often useful to transform scores into **standard scores** (otherwise known as *z-scores*). This is done by using deviations expressed in terms of standard deviation units:

$$\text{standard score } (z) = \frac{\text{deviation score } (x)}{\text{standard deviation (SD)}}$$

where $x = X - \bar{X}$.

When all scores in a set of scores are transformed into *z*-scores the distribution is said to be standardized. This point is returned to in the next chapter.

## Correlation

Measures of central tendency and dispersion are ways of describing and summarizing sets of scores on a single variable. However, we may well have data on two or more variables and want to look at the relationship between scores on the different variables. Suppose we have both error and time scores on a particular task from a group of participants. It may be that those who are good at the task do it quickly and make few errors. Those who are poor at it take longer and make more errors. Or there might be an entirely different relationship between scores on the two variables. Those who do it quickly might make many errors. Those doing it slowly and carefully make few errors. Such relationships are known as **correlations** between scores on the two variables, i.e. they are co-relationships.

A **positive correlation** is when high scores on one variable tend to be paired with high scores on the second variable (e.g. when individuals make many errors and take a long time); and low scores on one variable tend to be paired with low scores on the other (e.g. when they make few errors and take a short time).

A **negative correlation** is when high scores on one variable tend to be paired with low scores on the second variable (e.g. when individuals make many errors and take a short time); and low scores on one variable tend to be paired with high scores on the other (e.g. when they make few errors and take a long time).

Various **correlation coefficients** have been devised which give a numerical value for the correlation. They give values ranging from +1 for a perfect positive correlation, through zero for no correlation, to −1 for a perfect negative correlation. Intermediate values give an indication of the strength of the relationship between the two variables. We will consider how one such coefficient can be calculated later in the chapter.

## Scattergrams

A simple and useful way of displaying the relationship between two variables is provided by the **scattergram** (sometimes referred to as a **scatterplot**). This involves plotting one of the variables along the horizontal dimension and the other along the vertical dimension. If the two variables are the independent variable and dependent variable in an experiment then the convention is to plot the independent variable on the horizontal axis, and the dependent variable on the vertical axis (this applies on all graphs).

However, in considering correlation, it may well be that both variables are dependent variables; or they may arise from some non-experimental situation where it is not appropriate to make the distinction between independent and dependent variables. Commonly scores arise from individuals being measured or otherwise contributing data on two variables, so that for each participant there is a pair of scores.

Suppose, for example, we obtain measures of height and weight for a class of children. To plot a scattergram each child contributes one dot, positioned according to their height and weight. Thus a subject with height 135 cm and weight 31 kg would be represented as shown in Figure 9.

For a set of subjects, the scattergram might look like Figure 10. This shows that there is some relationship between the variables. Tall children tend to be heavier. This is an example of a positive correlation, in that high scores on one of the variables (height) tend to be associated with high scores on the other variable (weight).

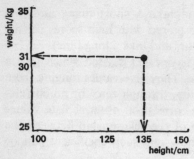

Figure 9    Representation on a scattergram of a participant with height 135 cm and weight 31 kg

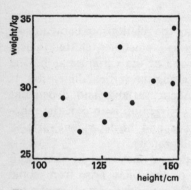

Figure 10    An example of a scattergram

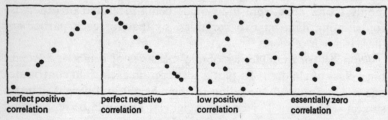

| perfect positive correlation | perfect negative correlation | low positive correlation | essentially zero correlation |

Figure 11    Scattergrams for different degrees of correlation

Examples of several different kinds of relationship are shown in Figure 11.

An alternative way of thinking about correlation is to say that a high or strong correlation enables us to make accurate predictions about an individual's score on one variable when we know their score on the other variable. Note that this applies with equal force for both positive and negative correlations. If there is a strong negative correlation, it simply means that we predict low scores for an individual on one variable if they score highly on the other variable.

## Spearman's rho

Several correlation coefficients have been developed. We will cover just one of these here, Spearman's rho ($\rho$), otherwise known as Spearman's rank order correlation coefficient. Appendix 2 gives details of a second correlation coefficient, Pearson's r.

Spearman's rho is based on rank orders. It deals, not with the scores themselves, but with the order of these scores when they have been ranked in size. There are, of course, some situations where ranks or orderings are all we have. Say that we can measure preferences within a set of things so that one of them is placed first (given rank one), another is placed second (given rank two) and so on. Spearman's rho can also be used in situations like this where the data are in the form of ranks from the start.

Suppose we have two people ranking a set of eight politicians on some quality, say honesty. The ranks may be as follows:

*Table 7* Rankings of politicians' honesty given by two persons

|  | Rank given to politician | | | | | | | |
| --- | --- | --- | --- | --- | --- | --- | --- | --- |
|  | *A* | *B* | *C* | *D* | *E* | *F* | *G* | *H* |
| person 1 | 1 | 2 | 3 | 4 | 5 | 6 | 7 | 8 |
| person 2 | 1 | 4 | 2 | 5 | 8 | 6 | 3 | 7 |

We have taken the first person's ordering as the basis and shown how the second person compares – thus they agree about who is most honest, but the politician ranked second by the first person is ranked fourth by the second person. In attempting to measure the correlation between these rankings it is clear that if they are perfectly correlated we have two possibilities. Either the rankings given by the two persons are identical (a perfect positive correlation); or one ranking is the reverse of the other. Whoever person one ranks first is ranked last by person two, and so on (a perfect negative correlation).

Spearman's rho is based upon the amount of disagreement between the two rankings. Specifically, the measure used is the sum of the squared difference in ranks (i.e. $\Sigma d^2$, where $d$ is the difference in rankings for each of the things ranked).

In the example given above, $d = 0$ for politician A, $d = -2$ for politician B, $d = 1$ for politician C, etc. and

$$\Sigma d^2 = 0^2 + (-2)^2 + 1^2 + (-1)^2 + (-3)^2 + 0^2 + 4^2 + 1^2 = 32$$

It is clear that $\Sigma d^2$ will be a minimum, in fact zero, when the two rankings are identical. Similarly $\Sigma d^2$ will be a maximum when one rank order is the exact reverse of the other. Hence the equation

$$\text{Spearman's rho } (\rho) = 1 - \frac{2\,\Sigma d^2}{\text{maximum value of } \Sigma d^2}$$

gives a correlation coefficient of $+1$ when there is no disagreement ($\Sigma d^2 = 0$) and a correlation coefficient of $-1$ where the disagreement is a maximum. You can check this by substituting $\Sigma d^2$ for 'maximum value of $\Sigma d^2$' into the equation for Spearman's rho.

It is not unreasonable to think of a total lack of correlation as being half-way between these two extremes of perfect agreement and perfect disagreement. If we take the value of $\Sigma d^2$ as half of its maximum value, you find that this produces a value of zero for Spearman's rho. If $\Sigma d^2$ is less than half of its maximum a positive correlation results; if more than half there will be a negative correlation.

While the equation given above is not difficult to use, a version which looks rather different is more commonly used. This relies on the fact that the maximum value of $\Sigma d^2$ can be worked out directly from $N$, the number of things ranked.

$$\text{Spearman's rho } (\rho) = 1 - \frac{6\, \Sigma d^2}{N(N^2 - 1)}$$

where $\Sigma d^2$ is the sum of squared differences in rank and $N =$ the number of pairs of ranks.

Note, by the way, that the '6' in the formula is, rather surprisingly, derived from the algebra, and is always there no matter how many pairs of scores you have.

Spearman's rho is a descriptive statistic. It simply describes and summarizes the direction and degree of the relationship between the variables. It is, however, possible to assess the statistical significance of the relationship between the variables in a similar way to that discussed with the sign test (p. 37). Table C gives figures for the smallest values of Spearman's rho significant at the 0·05 level of significance, for different numbers of pairs of scores.

If $\rho$ exceeds the table value for the number of pairs of scores in the experiment, then there is a statistically significant agreement between the rankings under the two conditions (at the $p = 0.05$ level). If $\rho$ does not exceed the table value, then there is no significant agreement between the rankings under the two conditions (at the $p = 0.05$ level).

## Step-by-step procedure

### Spearman's rho

**Step 1** Rank data (for each group separately) giving rank 1 to the highest score, and so on
*Note* If two or more scores in a group are the same then give the average rank for these tied scores

**Step 2** Obtain the difference ($d$) between each pair of ranks                $d$

**Step 3** Square each of the differences                $d^2$

**Step 4** Add all the squares together                $\Sigma d^2$

**Step 5** Calculate $N \times (N^2 - 1)$ where                $N(N^2 - 1)$
$N$ is the number of pairs of scores

**Step 6** $\rho = 1 - \dfrac{6\Sigma d^2}{N(N^2 - 1)}$

**Step 7** If required, assess the significance of $\rho$ using Table C

**Step 8** Translate the result back in terms of the experiment.

*Note* The procedure can be followed if the data is given directly in the form of ranks by simply omitting Step 1

## Worked example

### Spearman's rho

| Participant | Scores | |
| --- | --- | --- |
| | A | B |
| $P_1$ | 3 | 5 |
| $P_2$ | 7 | 9 |
| $P_3$ | 3 | 7 |
| $P_4$ | 12 | 11 |
| $P_5$ | 8 | 11 |
| $P_6$ | 14 | 11 |
| $P_7$ | 2 | 2 |

| Step 1 | ranks | | Step 2 | Step 3 |
| --- | --- | --- | --- | --- |
| Participant | A | B | d | $d^2$ |
| $P_1$ | 5·5 | 6 | −0·5 | 0·25 |
| $P_2$ | 4 | 4 | 0 | 0 |
| $P_3$ | 5·5 | 5 | 0·5 | 0·25 |
| $P_4$ | 2 | 2 | 0 | 0 |
| $P_5$ | 3 | 2 | 1 | 1 |
| $P_6$ | 1 | 2 | −1 | 1 |
| $P_7$ | 7 | 7 | 0 | 0 |

**Step 4** $\Sigma d^2 = 2 \cdot 50$

**Step 5** $N \times (N^2 - 1) = 7 \times (49 - 1) = 336$

**Step 6**

$$\rho = 1 - \frac{6 \, \Sigma \, d^2}{N(N^2 - 1)} = 1 - \frac{6 \times 2 \cdot 50}{336}$$

$$= 1 - 0 \cdot 045 = +0 \cdot 955$$

**Step 7** From Table C, $\rho$ must exceed 0·71 for $N = 7$. As $\rho = 0 \cdot 955$ there is a statistically significant agreement between the orderings of the data at the $p = 0 \cdot 05$ level

**Step 8** There is a statistically significant positive correlation ($\rho = +0 \cdot 955$) between the scores on the two variables

*Note* Spearman's rho should be treated with caution when there is a high proportion of ties as in this example

61

# 5 The normal distribution and distributions associated with it

We have made use of the histogram on several occasions so far to give a pictorial or graphical view of how a set of scores is distributed. Let us take as a further example the distribution of heights of children of a given age. This distribution might look something like Figure 12. Each bar of the histogram represents a height range of

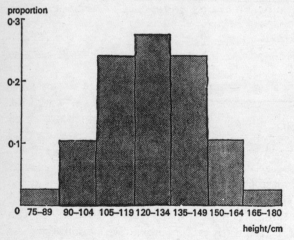

Figure 12 Histogram showing numbers of children with different heights

fifteen centimetres. There is no compelling reason why this range should be chosen. It could be smaller; indeed, the interval could be as small as one liked, providing that the measurements were sufficiently sensitive. (It only makes sense to do this when drawing a histogram if you have a large enough sample to ensure that the

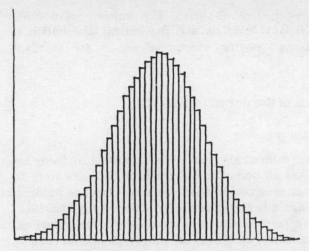

Figure 13 Approximation of a histogram to a smooth curve as the interval decreases

frequency or number of cases in different categories still remains reasonably large.)

A variable of this type, which can be continuously sub-divided, is called a **continuous** variable. There are other types of variables. Ones which can only take on particular numerical values are called **discrete** variables (e.g. size of family). There are also non-numerical **categorical** variables (e.g. gender – female or male).

By reducing the size of the interval with a continuous variable, the rectangles increase in number and become thinner so that the histogram approximates to a smooth curve when there is a sufficiently large sample (Figure 13). One such curve which you will hear referred to frequently is the **normal distribution curve**. As its properties were first investigated by Gauss, it is also commonly known as the **Gaussian distribution**. Incidentally, there is nothing abnormal or peculiar about other distribution curves – it just so happens that the so-called 'normal' curve is one which crops up many times and which has particularly useful, simple, and well-known mathematical properties. Different normal distributions vary only in their means and standard deviations and hence, if they are standardized so that they have the same mean and standard deviation, they have identical shapes. This intimate relationship between the standard deviation and the normal distribution is one of the reasons for the widespread use of the standard deviation.

## The importance of the normal distribution

### 1 On theoretical grounds

It can be shown theoretically that, if we assume that there are many small effects all operating independently of each other to influence a particular score or other outcome, then the resulting distribution of scores is the normal distribution. As we have discussed previously, performance in an experiment is conceptualized as resulting from a large number of separate random errors arising from uncontrolled variables, in addition to the possible effect of the independent variable.

### 2 On practical grounds

If a sufficiently large number of observations or measurements are made so that the shape of the distribution can be assessed it will very frequently transpire that the distribution does actually approximate more or less closely to the normal distribution. For example, human height is distributed in this way (providing you control for gender and ethnic background – a distribution with both males and females would be bimodal – see p. 43). So is human intelligence as measured by IQ tests, although this tells us more about the standardization procedures used than anything else.

### 3 On mathematical grounds

It has already been pointed out that the normal distribution is particularly simple mathematically. It is also very useful that the results obtained by assuming a normal distribution are often applicable even when the distribution differs somewhat from the normal.

## The shape of the normal distribution curve

The shape of the normal distribution curve is illustrated in Figure 14. It is bell-shaped and is symmetrical about its mean. In other words, if one imagines a vertical line drawn through the mean, then the shapes on either side of the line are identical. The median and mode occur at the same value as the mean. The curve falls away relatively slowly at first on either side of the mean, i.e. there

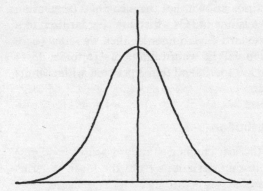

Figure 14   The normal distribution curve

is a high probability of scores occurring just a little above or just a little below the mean. When one gets to the 'tail' of the distribution, either above or below the mean, the curve approaches the horizontal axis 'asymptotically'. That is, the slope of the curve decreases continually for values further and further from the mean so that although the axis is approached it is never actually reached (although this is impossible to show on a drawing such as Figure 14). What this means is that there will be some very small probability of getting values a long way from the mean.

The standard deviation is associated with the curve in the following way. If we consider an upper limit obtained by going one standard deviation above the mean, and a lower limit obtained by going one standard deviation below the mean, a certain proportion of the cases, scores or whatever makes up the distribution, will be contained within these limits. For all normal distributions, this proportion is 0·6826, that is 68·26 per cent of the scores in any normal distribution fall within the limits of one standard deviation above and below the mean. In other words just over two-thirds of the scores are within a standard deviation of the mean.

If we consider wider limits, say two standard deviations above and below the mean, then the shape of the normal distribution is such that 95·44 per cent of the scores fall within these limits. For plus and minus three standard deviations, this percentage rises to 99·73 per cent.

To take an example: if it is known that the mean of a population is 100 (say the population is one of IQs which are standardized to a mean of 100) and the standard deviation is 15, then we know 68·26 per cent of the population will lie within limits of 115 to 85; 95·44 per cent within limits of 130 to 70; and 99·73 per cent within limits of 145 to 55.

## Standard normal distribution

As was pointed out in the last chapter, standard scores (z-scores) can be obtained by expressing deviations from the mean in terms of standard deviation units,

i.e. standard score $z = \dfrac{\text{deviation score } x}{\text{standard deviation}}$

Tables of the normal distribution are usually given in this standard form. Table D (p. 163) is an example which shows the fractional area under the standard normal curve. It can be seen from this table that for a z-score of 1·0, the fractional area enclosed between the mean of the distribution (where $z = 0$) and $z = 1·0$ is 0·3413. Figure 15 illustrates this.

As the curve is symmetrical, the area enclosed between z-scores of $-1·0$ and $+1·0$ is therefore $2 \times 0·3413 = 0·6826$. Another way of expressing this is to say that a proportion of 0·6826 (i.e. 68·26 per cent) is contained within these limits – which is what was stated in the last section.

Taking a different example of the use of Table D, look at the area corresponding to a z-score of 1·96. The table shows that this is

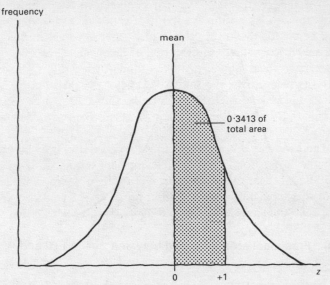

frequency

mean

0·3413 of
total area

0          +1                    z

Figure 15    Fractional area enclosed between $z = 0$ and
$z = +1$

0·4750. Therefore between the limits of $z = -1·96$ and $z = +1·96$
a fractional area of $2 \times 0·4750 = 0·95$ (95 per cent) is contained.
This means, of course, that 5 per cent of the population exceeds
these limits. Figure 16 shows this.

Hence, in an experimental situation where we can establish that
we are dealing with the normal distribution, a $z$-score exceeding
1·96 can be used to demonstrate that the IV had an effect on the
DV at the 5 per cent level of significance. Use the table to find the
$z$-score corresponding to the 1 per cent level of significance.

## Samples and populations

In an experiment, what we are doing is collecting a set of scores.
Typically, these scores are considered as a sample taken from some
population. By appropriate randomization techniques, we try to
make sure that each member of the population has an equal chance

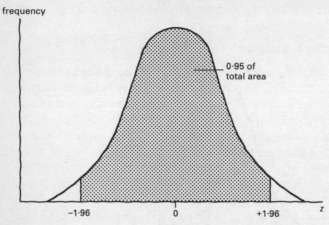

frequency

0·95 of
total area

−1·96          0          +1·96          z

Figure 16    Fractional area enclosed between $z = +1.96$ and
$z = -1.96$

of appearing in the sample. This then means that the results obtained from the sample can be generalized to the population.

You may be confused about the way in which we have been using the words 'sample' and 'population'. In statistics they are not limited to references to people. Thus, one talks about samples and populations of scores, as well as samples and populations of people.

When standard deviation was being discussed earlier, it was pointed out that the formula we used was appropriate for obtaining estimates of the population standard deviation from the scores in the sample. Thus, if from our sample we obtain a value of 80 for the mean and 10 for the standard deviation, then our estimate is that in the population from which the sample is drawn, 68 per cent of the scores will lie between the limits of 70 to 90.

This is only an estimate, of course. We have no certainty that it is correct. But it does mean that if, at a later stage, we obtain a score of 56 it would be quite improbable that it came from the same population (after all we estimate that approximately 95 per cent of the scores lie between 60 and 100, i.e. between plus and minus two standard deviations). It would not be impossible, however, for the score of 56 to come from the population – remember those tails approaching the horizontal axis asymptotically.

## Comparing two samples

A problem which we are much more likely to be concerned with in attempting to evaluate the results of our experiments is the decision as to whether the scores obtained under one experimental treatment or condition differ from the scores obtained under another experimental treatment or condition. We have already considered one way in which a decision could be reached – by using the sign test – but there ought to be a way which would make direct use of the actual scores which we obtain. What we would really like to know is whether the difference in the mean scores of the two experimental samples can be taken as evidence that there is a genuine difference between the two experimental conditions. The question is a familiar one: Is the observed difference in means sufficiently unlikely when random errors alone are involved that we are willing to decide that something else apart from the random errors is having an effect? In other words that the IV is affecting the DV?

In order to attack this problem, we have to consider a special kind of standard deviation called the **standard error**.

## Standard error

Suppose that we take as a population the actual population of male Chinese in the world. And further suppose that we take a random sample of 1000 of them and measure their heights. (The actual procedure necessary to get a random sample is left to the fertile imagination of the reader, as I am not sure that I could do it. Remember that each individual must have an equal chance of ending up in the sample.) The distribution might look something like Figure 17. Flushed by our success, we gather in a second sample of 1000 and measure again. This time we might find that the mean of the distribution was slightly higher. Repeating the process again with a third sample would lead to a slightly different mean again, and so on. The point I am trying to make is that we would not obtain identical means from successive samples. There

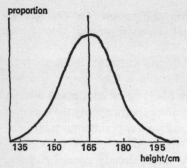

Figure 17   Distribution of heights for a sample of 1000 people (fictitious data)

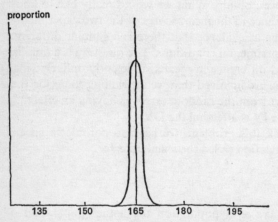

Figure 18   Distribution of *mean* heights of samples of 1000 people

would be a certain amount of variation. If one were to sample repeatedly in this way, taking 1000 people at a time, it would be possible to build up a **sampling distribution of the means**. This is a curve showing the frequency of occurrence of different mean scores, and it might look something like Figure 18. If this is compared with the sampling distribution of the scores themselves, it can be seen that there is much less variability in the mean scores than in the individual scores. An alternative way of putting this is to say that the standard deviation of the means is considerably less than the standard deviation of the scores themselves. *The standard deviation of the means is given a special name – the* **standard error**.

It is common sense that the means will vary much less than the individual scores. Mathematically there is a very simple and neat relationship between the standard error (SE) of the means, and the standard deviation (SD) of the scores:

$$SE = \frac{SD}{\sqrt{N}},$$

where $N$ is the size of sample (1000 in the example quoted above).

## The *t*-test

Let us say that, in an experiment, the mean score for condition A exceeded that for condition B, where A and B are two levels of a particular independent variable. Are we justified then in saying that the IV is affecting the DV? This is, once again, the question of generalizing from the sample of experimental results to the population. Two factors which would influence our decision are, firstly, the size of the difference in means and, secondly, the amount of variability in the scores. The bigger the difference in means, the more confidence we have that the sample difference reflects a real difference between the experimental conditions. But the larger the variability in scores, the less is our confidence.

These two factors are taken into account in the *t*-test, where

$$t = \frac{\text{difference in means}}{\text{standard error of the difference in means}}$$

Previously, we have talked about the standard error as being the name given to the standard deviation of the mean. This can be generalized to indicate the standard error of the difference in two means. If we draw two samples from a single population and look at the means of the two samples, we will find that almost always there will be some difference in the mean scores. Sometimes the difference will be negligible.

By taking repeated pairs of samples and each time noting the

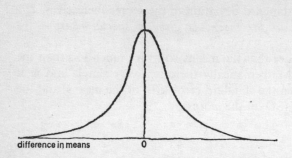

difference in means        0

Figure 19    Sampling distribution of difference in means of two samples taken from the same population

difference in the means of the two samples, it will be possible to plot the sampling distribution of the difference in means in a similar manner to that in which the sampling distribution of the means was built up in Figure 18. An example of what this might look like is shown in Figure 19.

By the way, do not worry that you are going to have to spend the rest of your life painstakingly building up sampling distributions by taking sample after sample. By using statistical theory it is possible, after making certain assumptions about the population and sample, to derive formulae for the sampling distributions.

Do not be confused by Figure 19 looking very different from Figure 18. By choosing an appropriate scale for Figure 19, both figures could be made to look very much the same. The point made by drawing Figures 17 and 18 to the same horizontal scale is that the sampling distribution of individual scores is much wider than the sampling distribution of mean scores. Similarly, the sampling distribution for difference in individual scores would be much wider than the sampling distribution for difference in means if it were drawn to the same horizontal scale as Figure 19.

It is perhaps surprising that if the samples drawn from the population are relatively small (say 50 or less) then the sampling distribution of $t$ is not normal, although the underlying population is itself normal. The distribution is known as the $t$-distribution and differs slightly in shape from the normal distribution. However, it

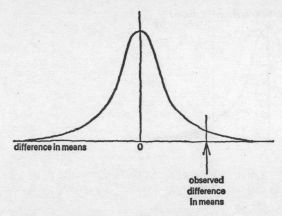

Figure 20    Observed difference in means superimposed on the sampling distribution of Figure 19

gets closer and closer to the normal distribution as the sample size increases.

Let us say that the observed difference in means in a particular experiment is as shown in Figure 20. If the samples had been drawn from the same populations this difference in means is unlikely to occur. As you can see, it takes us into one of the tails of the distribution. But is it sufficiently improbable for us to come to the decision that the independent variable did have an effect on the dependent variable?

The way in which we come to this decision is identical to the way in which we came to a decision for the sign test. We decide on a significance level. Remember that the significance level is the probability of making a type 1 error, i.e. the probability of deciding that the independent variable had an effect on the dependent variable when this is not the case. If we choose the conventional significance level of 5 per cent this amounts to cutting off 5 per cent of the *t*-distribution. This has been done in Figure 21. Here the distribution is divided into a central region, where the decision is made that the IV had no effect on the DV; and the two tails (shaded in the figure) where the decision is made that the IV did have an effect on the DV. What value of difference in means do we take as the critical value, i.e. the one which is exceeded by 5 per cent of the population? This is given, in terms of *t*, in Table E (p. 164).

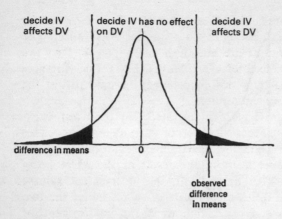

Figure 21    Cut-off points added to Figure 20

As discussed above, the $t$ statistic is the difference in means divided by the standard error. An alternative way of saying the same thing is by regarding it as a difference in means measured in units of standard error. A $t$ of 2 indicates that the difference in means is twice the standard error, and so on. A feature of the $t$-distribution is that it changes shape somewhat as the size of the sample changes. This means that the critical 5 per cent value changes with the sample size (which is related to the d.f. – degrees of freedom – of Table E).

## Computation of $t$

The computation of $t$ differs according to whether we are using an independent samples design on the one hand; or a matched pairs or repeated measures design on the other hand (see pp. 18–19).

## Assumptions underlying the $t$-test

In deriving the $t$-distribution, certain assumptions have to be made about the populations from which the samples are drawn. These are that the population distributions are **normal** and of the **same variance** (sometimes called the **homogeneity of variance** assumption). It is possible to test for the reasonableness of these assumptions for particular sets of scores. The **chi-square test** (Chapter 6) can be used as a test of 'goodness of fit' to a normal distribution. The details of how this is done are not given in Chapter 6. They are available in more advanced texts, e.g. Hayes (1981). The variance-ratio test (discussed later in this chapter) can be used to test the homogeneity of variance assumption.

However, statisticians have demonstrated that the $t$-test is extremely **robust** with respect to violation of these assumptions. This means there can be considerable deviation from normality and/or homogeneity of variance without the result of the $t$-test being affected. An exception to this is with the independent sample design when there are different numbers of scores under the two experimental conditions. Here, violations of the homogeneity of variance assumptions can be serious, and it is worthwhile to test this assumption (using the variance-ratio test) before carrying out the $t$-test.

The strategy recommended for all other cases is to examine the data and then, unless there are glaring deviations from either normality or from homogeneity of variance, go ahead with the $t$-test.

## One-tail and two-tail tests

There are some situations where we have a good reason for specifying the expected direction of the difference between the means (or, more generally, the direction of the effect of the IV). This reason may be theoretical, that is, it comes out as prediction from a theory. Or it may be from previous work done in the area, either by yourself or others. In some cases, it may simply be common sense. If, for example, you are working on some aspect of the abilities of persons who have recently suffered from strokes, it is a reasonable presupposition that they may be inferior to those of control non-stroke persons.

In situations such as this use can be made of what is called a **one-tailed test**. The reason for the name is obvious – we are dealing with only one of the tails of the distribution shown in Figure 21. In this case the null hypothesis that there is no difference in means is being tested against a directional alternative hypothesis where condition A (say) has a higher mean than condition B.

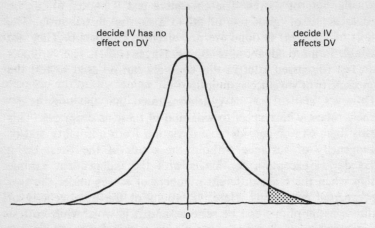

Figure 22    One-tailed test

We will, if we are using a one-tailed test, only decide that the IV has affected the DV if the experimental result falls at one end of the distribution – as illustrated in Figure 22.

The previous situation, as shown in Figure 21, is a **two-tailed test**. This is appropriate when the null hypothesis (of *no* difference) is being tested against a non-directional alternative hypothesis (simply that there *is* a difference).

There is an important difference in interpretation of significance levels for one-tailed and two-tailed tests. **The 5 per cent *t*-value for a two-tailed test becomes a 2·5 per cent value if a one-tailed test is used**. This is because the 5 per cent value in the table refers to 5 per cent of the distribution occurring in the two tails taken together; hence there is 2·5 per cent in each of the separate tails. So, if we wish to use the conventional 5 per cent significance level in conjunction with a one-tail test, we must use the 10 per cent value in the table. These values are not shown in Table E but are available in books of Statistical Tables.

It may have occurred to you that, because of this, it can happen that a result which would not be statistically significant if a two-tail test is used may become statistically significant if a one-tail test is used. Whilst this might seem somewhat fishy, remember that the decision about what kind of hypothesis you are dealing with should be made *before* doing the experiment and not after. There are people who argue that two-tailed tests should always be used and, starting out on experimentation as you are, it is wise to deal almost exclusively in terms of two-tailed tests. Remember that if you have a one-tailed test and the result comes out in the opposite direction to that hypothesized, then you cannot conclude that the IV had an effect on the DV, even in cases where the difference in means is large.

## Significance revisited

By this time you should be getting more of a feel of the meaning of statisical significance. If you are not you should skip back to p. 32 and review this. It is perhaps appropriate to add a word of warning here. In common usage 'significant' means something like 'important'. However, remember that statistical significance simply tells us that something is unlikely to have happened by chance. This in itself tells us little about the practical importance of the effect which we have found. In particular you should note that by increasing the sample size, that is by collecting more data, you are going to make it more likely to get a statistically significant result. This appears intuitively clear in the case of the $t$-test where increasing the sample size ($N$) has the effect of decreasing the standard error ($= SD/\sqrt{N}$) and hence of increasing the value of $t$ ($=$ difference in means/SE).

Another way of putting this is to appreciate that with a sufficiently large sample size one can get a significant value of $t$ with a very small difference in means. In practical terms this difference in means may be trivial, particularly if we have a complex situation where other variables are more important. So, the general message is that statistical significance is not all-important and, once again, that you cannot afford to switch off your common sense when interpreting the results of experiments.

## Step-by-step procedure

### *t*-Test – independent samples

Use with independent samples design
(NB **steps A1–5** and **B1–5** are identical to **steps 1–5** of the standard deviation procedure, p. 52.)

| | | |
|---|---|---|
| **Step A1** | Add all A observations together | $\Sigma X_A$ |
| **Step A2** | Divide **A1** (i.e. the result of **step A1**) by the number of A observations $N_A$ | $\dfrac{\Sigma X_A}{N_A} = \bar{X}_A$ |
| **Step A3** | (a) Square each of the A observations | $X_A^2$ |
| | (b) Add all the squares together | $\Sigma X_A^2$ |
| **Step A4** | (a) Square **A1** | $(\Sigma X_A)^2$ |
| | (b) Divide **A4a** by $N_A$ | $\dfrac{(\Sigma X_A)^2}{N_A}$ |
| **Step A5** | Subtract **A4b** from **A3b** | $\Sigma X_A^2 - \dfrac{(\Sigma X_A)^2}{N_A}$ |

**Steps B1–5** Repeat the above 5 steps for the B observations

## Worked example

### *t*-Test – independent samples

| | A observation | Step A3a $(A \text{ observation})^2$ | B observation |
|---|---|---|---|
| | 3 | 9 | 6 |
| | 5 | 25 | 5 |
| | 2 | 4 | 7 |
| | 4 | 16 | 8 |
| | 6 | 36 | 9 |
| | 2 | 4 | 4 |
| | 7 | 49 | 7 |
| | — | — | 8 |
| Step A1 $\Sigma X_A = 29$ | | Step A3b $\Sigma X_A^2 = 143$ | 9 |
| | | | 7 |

Step A2 $\bar{X}_A = \dfrac{29}{7} = 4.14$

Step A4a $(\Sigma X_A)^2 = 29^2$

Step A4b $\dfrac{(\Sigma X_A)^2}{N_A} = \dfrac{29^2}{7} = 120.1$

Step A5 $\Sigma X_A^2 - \dfrac{(\Sigma X_A)^2}{N_A} = 143 - 120.1 = 22.9$

Step B1 $\Sigma X_B = (6 + 5 + 7 + 8 + 9 + 4 + 7 + 8 + 9 + 7)$
$= 70$

Step B2 $\bar{X}_B = \dfrac{70}{10} = 7$

Step B3 $\Sigma X_B^2 = (36 + 25 + 49 + 64 + 81 + 16 + 49 + 64 + 81$
$+ 49) = 514$

Step B4a $(\Sigma X_B)^2 = 70^2$

Step B4b $\dfrac{(\Sigma X_B)^2}{N_B} = \dfrac{70^2}{10} = 490$

Step B5 $\Sigma X_B^2 - \dfrac{(\Sigma X_B)^2}{N_B} = 514 - 490 = 24$

## *t*-Test – independent samples

**Step 6** Add **A5** and **B5**

$$\left[\Sigma X_A^2 - \frac{(\Sigma X_A)^2}{N_A}\right] + \left[\Sigma X_B^2 - \frac{(\Sigma X_B)^2}{N_B}\right]$$

**Step 7** Divide **6** by $N_A$ minus 1 added to $N_B$ minus 1

$$\frac{[\Sigma X_A^2 - (\Sigma X_A)^2/N_A] + [\Sigma X_B^2 - (\Sigma X_B^2)/N_B]}{(N_A - 1) + (N_B - 1)}$$

**Step 8** Find the reciprocal of $N_A$ and the reciprocal of $N_B$ and add them together

$$\frac{1}{N_A} + \frac{1}{N_B}$$

**Step 9** Multiply **7** by **8**

$$\frac{[\Sigma X_A^2 - (\Sigma X_A)^2/N_A] + [\Sigma X_B^2 - (\Sigma X_B)^2/N_B]}{(N_A - 1) + (N_B - 1)} \times$$

$$\left(\frac{1}{N_A} + \frac{1}{N_B}\right)$$

**Step 10** Take the square root of **9**

**Step 11** Take the difference between **A2** and **B2**
$$\bar{X}_A - \bar{X}_B$$

**Step 12** Divide **11** by **10**: the result is *t*!!

$$t = (\bar{X}_A - \bar{X}_B)$$
$$\div \sqrt{\left[\frac{\{\Sigma X_A^2 - (\Sigma X_A)^2/N_A\} + \{\Sigma X_B^2 - (\Sigma X_B)^2/N_B\}}{(N_A - 1) + (N_B - 1)} \times \right.}$$
$$\left.\left(\frac{1}{N_A} + \frac{1}{N_B}\right)\right]$$

with $(N_A - 1) + (N_B - 1)$ degrees of freedom

**Step 13** Translate the result back in terms of the experiment

**Worked example – continued**

## *t*-Test – independent samples

**Step 6**   $22\cdot9 + 24 = 46\cdot9$

**Step 7**   $\dfrac{46\cdot9}{(7-1)+(10-1)} = \dfrac{46\cdot9}{15} = 3\cdot13$

**Step 8**   $(\frac{1}{7} + \frac{1}{10}) = (0\cdot1429 + 0\cdot1000) = 0\cdot2429$

**Step 9**   $3\cdot13 \times 0\cdot2429 = 0\cdot760$

**Step 10**   $\sqrt{0\cdot760} = 0\cdot872$

**Step 11**   $4\cdot14 - 7 = -2\cdot86$

**Step 12**   $t = -\dfrac{2\cdot86}{0\cdot872} = -3\cdot28$

with $(7-1)+(10-1) = 15$ degrees of freedom
From Table E, $t = 2\cdot13$ at the 0·05 level of significance
(i.e. $p = 5$ per cent) with 15 degrees of freedom

**Step 13**   We therefore conclude that the IV had an effect on the DV, as the observed value of $t$ is numerically greater than 2·13

## Step-by-step procedure

### t-Test – correlated samples

Use with matched pairs or repeated measures design

| | | |
|---|---|---|
| **Step 1** | Obtain the difference ($d$) between each pair of scores | $d = (X_A - X_B)$ |
| **Step 2** | Add all the differences together | $\Sigma d$ |
| **Step 3** | Divide 2 (i.e. the result of **step 2**) by the number of pairs of scores ($n$) | $\dfrac{\Sigma d}{n} = \bar{d}$ |
| **Step 4** | (a) Square each of the differences<br>(b) Add all the squares together | $d^2$<br>$\Sigma d^2$ |
| **Step 5** | (a) Square **2** | $(\Sigma d)^2$ |
| | (b) Divide **5a** by $n$ | $\dfrac{(\Sigma d)^2}{n}$ |
| **Step 6** | Subtract **5b** from **4b** | $\Sigma d^2 - \dfrac{(\Sigma d)^2}{n}$ |
| **Step 7** | Divide **6** by $n(n-1)$ | $\dfrac{\Sigma d^2 - (\Sigma d)^2/n}{n(n-1)}$ |
| **Step 8** | Take the square root of **7** | |
| **Step 9** | Divide **3** by **8**: the result is $t$ | |

$$t = \bar{d} \div \sqrt{\dfrac{\Sigma d^2 - (\Sigma d)^2/n}{n(n-1)}}$$

with ($n-1$) degrees of freedom

**Step 10** Translate the result of the test back in terms of the experiment

# Worked example

## *t-Test – correlated samples*

The data represents scores obtained by 7 people in a certain test
with and without the presence of a drug

| Partici-<br>pant | Scores<br>with | Scores<br>without | **Step 1**<br>$d$ | **Step 4a**<br>$d^2$ |
|---|---|---|---|---|
| 1 | 3 | 6 | 3 | 9 |
| 2 | 8 | 14 | 6 | 36 |
| 3 | 4 | 8 | 4 | 16 |
| 4 | 6 | 4 | −2 | 4 |
| 5 | 9 | 16 | 7 | 49 |
| 6 | 2 | 7 | 5 | 25 |
| 7 | 12 | 19 | 7 | 49 |

**Step 2**   $\Sigma d = 30$

**Step 3**   $\dfrac{\Sigma d}{n} = \bar{d} = \dfrac{30}{7} = 4\cdot29$

**Step 4b**   $\Sigma d^2 = 188$

**Step 5a**   $(\Sigma d)^2 = 30^2 = 900$

**Step 5b**   $\dfrac{(\Sigma d)^2}{n} = \dfrac{900}{7} = 128\cdot57$

**Step 6**   $\Sigma d^2 - \dfrac{(\Sigma d)^2}{n} = 188 - 128\cdot57 = 59\cdot43$

**Step 7**   $\dfrac{\Sigma d^2 - (\Sigma d)^2/n}{n(n-1)} = \dfrac{59\cdot43}{7\times6} = 1\cdot41$

**Step 8**   $\sqrt{1\cdot41} = 1\cdot19$

**Step 9**   $t = \bar{d} \div \sqrt{\dfrac{\Sigma d^2 - (\Sigma d)^2/n}{n(n-1)}} = \dfrac{4\cdot29}{1\cdot19} = 3\cdot61$

with $(7 - 1) = 6$ degrees of freedom
From Table E, $\underline{t = 2\cdot45}$ at the 0·05 level of significance,
with 6 degrees of freedom

**Step 10** We therefore conclude that the IV had an effect on the
DV, as the observed $t$ is numerically greater than 2·45: the
drug produced a significant decrease in mean score on this
test ($t = 3\cdot61$ with 6 d.f. Significant at the 5 per cent level)

## The variance-ratio test (*F*-test)

In the discussion above, we have been concerned with hypotheses about differences in means between two conditions. Although many behavioural hypotheses can be translated into statistical hypotheses about means, there are others where the appropriate statistical hypothesis is concerned with the relative dispersion of scores under two conditions. The variance-ratio test (or *F*-test) is suitable for these situations.

(What is variance? If you have forgotten or are not sure return to p. 48.)

As an example, consider performance in some task with the preferred hand as against the non-preferred hand. Suppose we get our participants to play shove ha'penny with the preferred hand on some occasions, the non-preferred hand on others. One obvious way of comparing performance with the two hands would be by comparing the variability in aiming by the two hands, i.e. by using the variance-ratio test to compare the two variances.

You should note that the values shown in Table F relate to significance for a two-tailed test. Many books of tables give values for a one-tailed test which are appropriate for other uses of the variance-ratio test.

## Assumptions underlying the variance-ratio test

As with the *t*-test, the variance-ratio test makes assumptions about the underlying population distribution. Again the assumption is of normality. However, once again, the test is robust and the recommended action is to carry on with the variance-ratio test unless the distributions are very far from normal.

## Step-by-step procedure

### Variance-ratio test (F-test)

**Step 1** Obtain the variance separately for each set of scores (use the standard deviation step-by-step procedure as far as **step 6**; see p. 52)

**Step 2** Obtain $F = \dfrac{\text{larger variance}}{\text{smaller variance}}$

**Step 3** Look up the significance of $F$ in Table F. Note that you need two sets of degrees of freedom to do this. The columns in the table refer to the degrees of freedom of the top line of $F$ ($N_1 = N_A - 1$, where $N_A$ is the number of scores making up the larger variance). The rows in the table refer to the degrees of freedom of the bottom line of $F$ ($N_2 = N_B - 1$, where $N_B$ is the number of scores making up the smaller variance)

**Step 4** Translate the results of the test back in terms of the experiment

*Note* The values in Table F are appropriate for a two-tail test (i.e. testing for a difference in the variances without *a priori* specifying the direction of the difference). Many tables of $F$ refer to a one-tail test, which is useful in a different application of $F$

# Worked example

## Variance-ratio test (*F*-test)

The following error scores were obtained in an aiming test
*Non-preferred hand* (A): 3·3, 2·1, 4·7, 0·1, 5·6, 0·0, 4·7
*Preferred hand* (B): 5·6, 4·9, 6·2, 5·1, 5·8, 6·3

**Step 1** (using the method on p. 52)

| $X_A$ | (3a) $X_A^2$ |
|------|------|
| 3·3 | 10·89 |
| 2·1 | 4·41 |
| 4·7 | 22·09 |
| 0·1 | 0·01 |
| 5·6 | 31·36 |
| 0·0 | 0·00 |
| 4·7 | 22·09 |

| $X_B$ | (3a) $X_B^2$ |
|------|------|
| 5·6 | 31·36 |
| 4·9 | 24·01 |
| 6·2 | 38·44 |
| 5·1 | 26·01 |
| 5·8 | 33·64 |
| 6·3 | 39·69 |

**(1)** $\Sigma X_A = 20·5$  **(3b)** $\Sigma X_A^2 = 90·85$

**(2)** $\bar{X}_A = \dfrac{20·5}{7} = 2·93$

**(4a)** $(\Sigma X_A)^2 = 20·5^2 = 420·25$

**(4b)** $\dfrac{(\Sigma X_A)^2}{N_A} = \dfrac{420·25}{7} = 60·04$

**(5)** $\Sigma X_A^2 - \dfrac{(\Sigma X_A)^2}{N_A} = 90·85 - 60·04$
$$= 30·81$$

**(6)** $\text{variance}_A = \dfrac{30·81}{6} = \underline{5·14}$

**(1)** $\Sigma X_B = 33·9$  **(3b)** $\Sigma X_B^2 = 193·15$

**(2)** $\bar{X}_B = \dfrac{33·9}{6} = 5·65$

**(4a)** $(\Sigma X_B)^2 = 33·9^2 = 1149·21$

**(4b)** $\dfrac{(\Sigma X_B)^2}{N_B} = \dfrac{1149·21}{6} = 191·54$

**(5)** $\Sigma X_B^2 - \dfrac{(\Sigma X_B)^2}{N_B} = 193·15 - 191·54$
$$= 1·61$$

**(6)** $\text{variance}_B = \dfrac{1·61}{5} = \underline{0·322}$

**Step 2** $F = \dfrac{5·14}{0·322} = 15·9$

**Step 3** $N_1 = N_A - 1 = 6;$  $N_2 = N_B - 1 = 5$
Table value of $F = 6·98$ ($p = 0·05$)
As the observed value of $F$ exceeds the table value, there is a significant difference between the variances at the 5 per cent level

**Step 4** Inspection of the results shows that the variance for the non-preferred hand exceeds that for the preferred hand. This difference is significant at the 5 per cent level

# 6   Chi square

The chi-square techniques to be introduced in this chapter are appropriate for use with data in the form of **frequencies**. In other words, they deal with the situation where we are simply counting the number of times something occurs. This happens, for example, if a test is made of the effectiveness of a new teaching method, and the information available is whether students pass or fail a test after the teaching experience. We would then be able to count the number of passes and of failures for the new method and might compare these with the number of passes and failures of another group taught by the old method (for this to be a true experiment it would be necessary for students to be randomly allocated to the two conditions).

Data in the form of measurements (e.g. of height) such as were used in the *t*-test described in the last chapter would not be appropriate for chi square. However, it may be possible to convert measures into counts, by appropriate grouping, so that chi square is appropriate. For example, if heights of a group of subjects are available, they could be converted into counts of how many are *tall* (say over 180 cm), how many *medium* (180–165 cm) and how many *short* (under 165 cm). Some detailed information is, of course, lost by this procedure, but it may be that the experimental hypothesis can still be adequately tested by the frequency data.

## The 2 × 2 contingency table

In studying the possible relationship between smoking and lung cancer the data of Table 8 were obtained (fictitious data, if it is any comfort for smokers). This is an example of a 2 × 2 contingency table – sometimes called a fourfold table.

*Table 8* Smokers and non-smokers having cancer or not having cancer (fictitious data)

|  | Smokers | Non-smokers |  |
| --- | --- | --- | --- |
| cancer | 23 | 3 | 26 |
| no cancer | 465 | 652 | 1117 |
|  | 488 | 655 | 1143 |

It shows in compact form that, of an overall total of 1143 persons in the study, 488 were smokers and 655 were non-smokers. Of the smokers, 23 had developed lung cancer by a certain age, 465 had not. Of the non-smokers, 3 had developed lung cancer and 652 had not. We want to know if smokers are more likely to get cancer. We can see, of course, that the proportion of smokers developing cancer in our sample (23 out of 488 – just less than 5 per cent) is greater than the proportion of non-smokers developing cancer (3 out of 655 – less than $\frac{1}{2}$ per cent). But what we need to find out is how unlikely it is to get a difference in the proportions as large as is found here if only random effects are present.

The chi-square technique can be used to test the statistical significance of the difference in proportions. It can also be thought of in a rather different way – as a test of association between the categories used. Is smoking associated with lung cancer? Put more accurately, does membership of a given category on one dimension (e.g. smokers on the smoking/non-smoking dimension) tend to be associated with membership of a given category on the other dimension (e.g. lung cancer sufferers on the cancer/no-cancer dimension)?

If there is no association between the categories, the frequencies which would be expected can be worked out for each of the four 'cells' in the 2 × 2 table. As 26 persons develop lung cancer out of a total of 1143 (smokers and non-smokers together), one would expect that, *with no association*, the same proportion of smokers would develop cancer. So, of the 488 smokers, we expect that the proportion of $\frac{26}{1143}$ would develop cancer, i.e.

Expected number of smokers developing cancer = $488 \times \dfrac{26}{1143}$
(if no association)

$$= 11 \cdot 10$$

As 1117 out of 1143 overall do not develop the disease, we expect that with no association, this same proportion of the 488 smokers would escape, i.e.

Expected number of smokers not developing cancer = $488 \times \dfrac{1117}{1143}$
(if no association)

$$= 476 \cdot 90$$

Expected frequencies can be worked out in the same way for the other two cells in the table (try it). A general formula, which can be used for computing the expected frequency for a cell, is

**Expected frequency ($E$)** $= \dfrac{\textbf{row total} \times \textbf{column total}}{\textbf{overall total}}$

The table of expected frequencies is shown in Table 9.

*Table 9* Expected frequencies calculated from the data of Table 8, on the basis of no association between the categories.

|  | *Smokers* | *Non-smokers* |
|---|---|---|
| cancer | 11·10 | 14·90 |
| no cancer | 476·90 | 640·10 |

The chi-square statistic ($\chi^2$) can be computed from the actual frequencies obtained, usually called the observed frequencies ($O$) and the expected frequencies ($E$), using the formula

chi square (for 2 × 2 table) $\chi^2 = \Sigma \dfrac{(O - E)^2}{E}$

Here, the $\Sigma$ refers to 'taking the sum of' the contributions from each of the four cells in the table.

In each cell the difference between observed and expected frequencies is obtained and then squared. Note that the squared difference is, of course, positive even when the expected frequency is larger than the observed frequency. This square is then divided by the expected frequency for that cell. The sum of these values for each of the cells is $\chi^2$. You can see that the bigger the differences between $O$ and $E$ the bigger is $\chi^2$. Hence a sufficiently large value of $\chi^2$ leads to us accepting that there is a statistically significant association between the categories. Or, putting it in other words, that there is a statistically significant difference in proportions; one which is sufficiently unlikely to be due to random errors for us to reject the null hypothesis.

In our example,

$$\chi^2 = \Sigma \frac{(23 - 11 \cdot 10)^2}{11 \cdot 10} + \frac{(3 - 14 \cdot 90)^2}{14 \cdot 90}$$

$$+ \frac{(465 - 476 \cdot 90)^2}{476 \cdot 90} + \frac{(652 - 640 \cdot 10)^2}{640 \cdot 10}$$

$$= 12 \cdot 76 + 9 \cdot 50 + 0 \cdot 30 + 0 \cdot 22$$

$$= 22 \cdot 78$$

This can be assessed for significance by using Table G. However, in order to use this table, one has to know the appropriate degrees of freedom.

## Degrees of freedom

In obtaining the expected frequencies, the column and row totals (and hence the overall total) are taken as fixed. This means that when one of the expected frequencies has been computed, the rest can be found by subtraction from the marginal totals. The implication of this is that a $2 \times 2$ table of this type has only one 'degree of freedom', i.e. only one of the frequencies can be considered as free to vary if we are to ensure that the marginal totals add up to the right value. Thus, from Table G, the table value is

$$\chi^2 = 3 \cdot 841$$

with 1 degree of freedom (1 d.f.), at the 5 per cent level.

We now go through the sub-routine which you should be familiar with from all the tests we have dealt with so far. As the $\chi^2$ computed from the data exceeds the table value of $\chi^2$ for the 5 per cent level, we have evidence that the IV has affected the DV. In other words that there is a statistically significant association between the IV (smoking or not smoking) and the DV (incidence of lung cancer).

Note that the table for $\chi^2$ refers to the one-tailed test. This is appropriate for all the applications of $\chi^2$ referred to in this chapter. We are concerned with just one tail (the upper tail) of the chi-square distribution because large discrepancies between observed and expected frequencies are reflected in large values of $\chi^2$. These take us into that upper tail. The lower tail of the $\chi^2$ distribution corresponds to observed and expected frequencies being closer together than is likely on a chance basis, which is not usually of experimental interest.

This is a rather different issue from that covered in the earlier discussion of one- and two-tailed tests (p. 75). There, the one-tailed test was concerned with situations where we start out by predicting the direction of the difference between two conditions, and need to have a very good reason for using it instead of the two-tailed test. With $\chi^2$ the one-tailed test is the norm and simply refers to large differences between observed and expected frequencies, irrespective of the direction of the association.

## Chi square and small samples

As the chi-square function is a continuous curve and the observed frequencies used in its estimation must take on whole number values, the actual sampling distribution is only approximated by the continuous function.

The smaller the sample size, the worse is the fit to a continuous distribution and below a certain size $\chi^2$ should not be used. Although statisticians differ on the exact number below which $\chi^2$ should not be used, a simple rule of thumb is: **do not use chi square if one or more of the *expected* frequencies falls below five**. Note that this is the expected rather than the observed frequency. In the smoking and lung cancer example it is permissible to use $\chi^2$ because, although one of the observed frequencies is under five, all expected frequencies are above five.

An alternative small-sample test for data in the form of frequencies is called **Fisher's exact test**. This test can be used whatever the expected frequencies and is found in more advanced texts, such as Siegel and Castellan (1988).

## Independence of observations

There are probably more inappropriate and incorrect uses of the chi-square test than of all the other statistical tests put together. For one thing it should only be used appropriately if each and every observation is independent of each and every other observation. Violations of this rule are very common. If, for example, we use a repeated measures design where participants are categorized as successful or not on some test before and after the experimental task, then we have pairs of scores rather than independent ones; and $\chi^2$ should not be used.

In order to use $\chi^2$ appropriately, each observation has to qualify for one and only one cell in the table. Another common misuse of the statistic occurs when an attempt is made to leave out some of the observations. Suppose, for example, that we have 'high', 'medium' and 'low' categories of performance on a task; then it is inappropriate to simply select out two of the categories for analysis. The frequencies in each of the categories must be included in the $\chi^2$ analysis (a larger table than the $2 \times 2$ table will be needed, as discussed later in the chapter).

## Interpretation of the result of a chi-square test

A statistically significant $\chi^2$ is evidence for an association. Inspection of the data given above shows that the direction of this association is such that smokers are more likely to get lung cancer than non-smokers. Put differently, the proportion of smokers who get cancer (0·047) is significantly higher than the proportion of non-smokers who get cancer (0·005).

It is, of course, in attempting to interpret this result that we have to exercise caution. No details were given about the kind of study from which the data were obtained. We can safely assume that it was not a true experiment as this would have involved random assignment of persons to the 'smoking' and 'non-smoking' categories. Such an experiment would involve something like randomly assigning half of a group of non-smokers to begin smoking regularly. The ethics of that kind of study are, to say the least, somewhat dubious. However, in its absence, we are certainly in no position to say 'smoking *causes* lung cancer'.

Without random assignment there may well be many factors or variables which influence the outcomes of a study. As is well known, the existence of a causal relationship has been hotly disputed by many smokers and by cigarette manufacturers. One suggestion has been that people of a certain personality type are more like to smoke *and also* have cancer. Put more generally, the argument is that there is a third variable (personality type) which is associated with both the others.

This example can stand as a warning of the difficulties in interpreting the results of a statistical test. These difficulties are by no means restricted to $\chi^2$, but they often crop up in a particularly awkward form with this test.

## Step-by-step procedure

### 2 × 2 Chi square (test of association)

Use this test for *frequency data* only, i.e. for *counts* of different types of 'events'

---

**Step 1** Draw up the 2 × 2 table, making sure that each event goes into one of the cells and into not more than one cell. The number in each cell is the **observed frequency** $O$ for that cell

**Step 2** Find the row totals, column totals and grand total

**Step 3** Work out the **expected frequency** $E$ for each cell separately using the formula

$$E = \frac{\text{row total} \times \text{column total}}{\text{grand total}}$$

Put the expected frequency for each cell into that cell

## Worked example

### 2 × 2 Chi square (test of association)

A psychologist studying the symptoms of a random sample of 25 psychotics and 25 neurotics found that only 5 of the psychotics had suicidal feelings, whereas 12 of the neurotics had. Is there evidence for an association between the two psychiatric groups and the presence or absence of suicidal feelings?

**Step 1**

|  | Psychotics | Neurotics |
|---|---|---|
| suicidal | 5 | 12 |
| non-suicidal | 20 | 13 |

**Step 2**

|  |  |  |
|---|---|---|
| 5 | 12 | 17 |
| 20 | 13 | 33 |
| 25 | 25 | 50 |

**Step 3** For top left cell (cell A)    $E = \dfrac{17 \times 25}{50} = 8\cdot5$

For top right cell (cell B)    $E = \dfrac{17 \times 25}{50} = 8\cdot5$

For bottom left cell (cell C)    $E = \dfrac{33 \times 25}{50} = 16\cdot5$

For bottom right cell (cell D)    $E = \dfrac{33 \times 25}{50} = 16\cdot5$

|  |  |  |
|---|---|---|
| 8·5 <br> 5 | 8·5 <br> 12 | 17 |
| 16·5 <br> 20 | 16·5 <br> 13 | 33 |
| 25 | 25 | 50 |

## Step-by-step procedure – continued

### 2 × 2 Chi square (test of association)

**Step 4** Work out the difference between $O$ and $E$ for each cell.

**Step 5** Square this for each cell $(O - E)^2$

**Step 6** Divide by the appropriate $E$ value for that cell
$$\frac{(O - E)^2}{E}$$

**Step 7** Obtain $\chi^2$ by adding all these contributions from the different cells

$$\chi^2 = \Sigma \frac{(O - E)^2}{E}$$

This has 1 degree of freedom

**Step 8** If the $\chi^2$ obtained exceeds the table value (found in Table G) at the chosen level of significance, then there is evidence for an association between the categories

**Step 9** Translate the result of the test back in terms of your experiment

## Worked example – continued

### $2 \times 2$ Chi square (test of association)

|  | Step 4<br>$(O - E)$ | Step 5<br>$(O - E)^2$ |
|---|---|---|
| CELL A | $(5 - 8{\cdot}5) = -3{\cdot}5$ | $(-3{\cdot}5)^2 = 12{\cdot}25$ |
| CELL B | $(12 - 8{\cdot}5) = 3{\cdot}5$ | $3{\cdot}5^2 = 12{\cdot}25$ |
| CELL C | $(20 - 16{\cdot}5) = 3{\cdot}5$ | $3{\cdot}5^2 = 12{\cdot}25$ |
| CELL D | $(13 - 16{\cdot}5) = -3{\cdot}5$ | $(-3{\cdot}5)^2 = 12{\cdot}25$ |

**Step 6**

$$\frac{(O - E)^2}{E}$$

| CELL A | $12{\cdot}25/\ 8{\cdot}5 = 1{\cdot}4412$ |
|---|---|
| CELL B | $12{\cdot}25/\ 8{\cdot}5 = 1{\cdot}4412$ |
| CELL C | $12{\cdot}25/16{\cdot}5 = 0{\cdot}7424$ |
| CELL D | $12{\cdot}25/16{\cdot}5 = 0{\cdot}7424$ |

**Step 7**
$$\chi^2 = \Sigma \frac{(O - E)^2}{E}$$

$$= 1{\cdot}4412 + 1{\cdot}4412 + 0{\cdot}7424 + 0{\cdot}7424$$
$$= 4{\cdot}3672$$
$$= 4{\cdot}37 \text{ with 1 d.f.}$$

**Step 8** From Table G,
$\chi^2 = 3{\cdot}84$
with 1 d.f., at the 5 per cent significance level

**Step 9** There is significant evidence for an association between psychotism/neuroticism and presence/absence of suicidal feelings at the conventional (5 per cent) significance level (or *alternatively*, the proportion of psychotics with suicidal feelings differs significantly from the proportion of neurotics with suicidal feelings)

## Chi square in larger tables

Chi square can be used in tables with more than two rows and more than two columns. As with the 2 × 2 Chi square it can be regarded as a test of association between the attributes which make up the rows and those which make up the columns. The $\chi^2$ formula is the same. Thus,

$$\chi^2 = \Sigma \frac{(O - E)^2}{E}.$$

As before, the summation sign indicates that the quantities

$$\frac{(O - E)^2}{E},$$

having been computed for each cell, should be added together for all the cells.

The calculation of expected frequencies is as for the 2 × 2 table, i.e.

$$E = \frac{\text{row total} \times \text{column total}}{\text{overall total}},$$

the reasoning behind this being exactly the same as for the 2 × 2 case.

The number of degrees of freedom can also be arrived at as in the 2 × 2 case. If the row totals are considered fixed, then the frequencies in one cell in any row is fixed when values have been given to frequencies of the other cells. The same applies to the columns, so that in a table with $R$ rows and $C$ columns, the total number degrees of freedom is

$$(R - 1) \times (C - 1).$$

This is perhaps clearer when displayed. Figure 23 shows it for a 3 × 4 table and a 2 × 6 table. When values have been given to the frequencies of the unshaded cells then, given fixed marginal totals, the values of frequencies for each of the shaded cells can be computed:

for the 3 × 4 table
degrees of freedom = $(3 - 1) \times (4 - 1) = 6$

and for the 2 × 6 table
degrees of freedom = $(2 - 1) \times (6 - 1) = 5$.

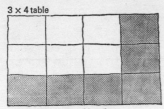

2 × 3 = 6 degrees of freedom

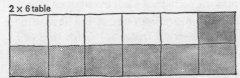

1 × 5 = 5 degrees of freedom

Figure 23   Degrees of freedom in large $\chi^2$ tables

In interpreting larger tables it may be helpful to convert the observed cell frequencies into proportions. Table 10 shows this for the data in the worked example on p. 103.

*Table 10* Contingency table with observed frequencies expressed as proportions

|  | *Method A* | *Method B* | *Method C* | *Overall* |
|---|---|---|---|---|
| pass | $\frac{50}{55} = 0{\cdot}91$ | $\frac{42}{61} = 0{\cdot}69$ | $\frac{56}{64} = 0{\cdot}88$ | $\frac{148}{180} = 0{\cdot}82$ |
| fail | $\frac{5}{55} = 0{\cdot}09$ | $\frac{19}{61} = 0{\cdot}31$ | $\frac{8}{64} = 0{\cdot}13$ | $\frac{32}{180} = 0{\cdot}18$ |

However, while it is often easier to pick out what is happening from the proportions, remember that $\chi^2$ must be calculated from the frequencies themselves.

## Step-by-step procedure

### Chi-square – tables larger than 2 × 2 (test of association)

Use this test for *frequency data* only, i.e. for *counts* of different types of 'events'

---

**Step 1** Draw up the table, making sure that each event goes into one of the cells and into no more than one cell. The number in each cell is the **observed frequency** $O$ for that cell

**Step 2** Find the row totals, column totals and grand total

**Step 3** Work out the **expected frequency** $E$ for each cell separately using the formula

$$E = \frac{\text{row total} \times \text{column total}}{\text{grand total}}$$

Put the expected frequency for each cell into that cell

## Worked example

### Chi square – tables larger than 2 × 2 (test of association)

In an exam, varying numbers of students passed and failed after having been taught by one of three different methods. It is required to test for an association between the numbers passing and failing and the method of instruction (i.e. does the relative proportion of passes differ from method to method?)

**Step 1**

|  | Method A | Method B | Method C |
|---|---|---|---|
| pass | 50 | 42 | 56 |
| fail | 5 | 19 | 8 |

**Step 2**

| | | | |
|---|---|---|---|
| 50 | 42 | 56 | 148 |
| 5 | 19 | 8 | 32 |
| 55 | 61 | 64 | 180 |

**Step 3** For top left-hand cell,

$$E = \frac{148 \times 55}{180} = 45.22$$

and so on for each of the cells:

| | | | |
|---|---|---|---|
| 45·22 50 | 50·16 42 | 52·62 56 | 148 |
| 9·78 5 | 10·84 19 | 11·38 8 | 32 |
| 55 | 61 | 64 | 180 |

## Step-by-step procedure – continued

## Chi-square – tables larger then 2 × 2 (test of association)

**Step 4**  Work out $(O - E)$ for each cell

**Step 5**  Square this for each cell

**Step 6**  Divide by the appropriate $E$ value for that cell

**Step 7**  Obtain $\chi^2$ by adding all these contributions from the different cells

**Step 8**  Obtain the degrees of freedom =
(number of rows $- 1$) × (number of columns $- 1$)

**Step 9**  If the $\chi^2$ obtained exceeds the table value (found in Table G) at the chosen level of significance, then there is evidence for an association between the categories

**Step 10**  Translate the result of the test back in terms of the experiment

## Worked example – continued

### Chi-square – tables larger than 2 × 2 (test of association)

| $O$ | $E$ | Step 4 $(O - E)$ | Step 5 $(O - E)^2$ | Step 6 $(O - E)^2/E$ |
|---|---|---|---|---|
| 50 | 45·22 | 4·78 | 22·85 | 0·505 |
| 42 | 50·16 | −8·16 | 66·59 | 1·328 |
| 56 | 52·62 | 3·38 | 11·42 | 0·217 |
| 5 | 9·78 | −4·78 | 22·85 | 2·336 |
| 19 | 10·84 | 8·16 | 66·59 | 6·143 |
| 8 | 11·38 | −3·38 | 11·42 | 1·004 |

**Step 7** $\chi^2 = \Sigma \dfrac{(O - E)^2}{E}$

$= 0{\cdot}505 + 1{\cdot}328 + 0{\cdot}217 + 2{\cdot}336 + 6{\cdot}143 + 1{\cdot}004$

$= 11{\cdot}53$

**Step 8** d.f. = (rows − 1) × (columns − 1) = 1 × 2 = 2

**Step 9** From Table G, $\chi^2 = 5{\cdot}99$ with 2 d.f. at the 5 per cent significance level. As the $\chi^2$ obtained (11·53) is greater than this table value, there is significant evidence for an association between the variables

**Step 10** There is significant evidence for an association between method of instruction and relative proportion of passes. In other words, the relative proportions of passes differ significantly from one method to another

*Note* That the significance applies to the data taken as a whole. However inspection of the table suggests that it is Method B which differs from the other two

## Small samples in larger tables

It is recommended that the same rule of thumb be applied as for small samples: **do not use chi square if one or more of the expected frequencies falls below five**.

This is a 'conservative' procedure in that circumstances may arise when the approximation to the chi-square distribution is adequate with smaller expected frequencies than this.

A common strategy when small expected frequencies are obtained is to pool categories in order to get the pooled expected frequencies above the magic number of five. There are difficulties in doing this, however. Possibly the hypothesis that one is interested in testing cannot be tested if categories are lumped together in this way. And even if this is still possible, a *post hoc* pooling (i.e. after the observed frequencies have been obtained) will affect the randomness of the sample. Exact tests exist as for the 2 × 2 case, but are difficult to compute for larger tables.

The obvious procedure to adopt is to take a large enough sample for the expected frequencies to be over five. If appropriate, categories can be combined in *a priori* fashion (i.e. before collecting the results). Finally, if one does end up with some low expected frequencies then it is probably preferable to go ahead with $\chi^2$ adding a caveat that there may be a relatively poor approximation to the exact probabilities.

## Chi square as a test of goodness of fit

We have so far considered $\chi^2$ as a test of association. When used in this way the expected frequencies are calculated directly from the observed frequencies by assuming independence between the categories. It is also possible to use $\chi^2$ in a rather different way where the expected frequencies are obtained from predictions based on theoretical considerations. When the $\chi^2$ statistic is computed in this way, it becomes a test of the **goodness of fit** between the observations and the theory.

Chi square can, for instance, be used to determine whether a given set of data may be regarded as a sample from a normal population, and hence to decide whether or not a particular statistical test which assumes a normal distribution could be validly used in some situation.

We will restrict ourselves in this chapter to a simple case which occurs quite frequently. This is where, in a single-row $\chi^2$, we are testing the hypothesis of equal probability of occurrence of the different alternatives (this is equivalent to testing the goodness of fit to a 'rectangular' distribution – a histogram of the distribution would be a rectangle with all the bars the same length). Thus, the expected frequency for each cell is obtained simply by dividing the total number of observations by the number of cells in the row. Degrees of freedom are one less than the number of cells, the reasoning being as before. The formula used is unchanged. The same rule of thumb for expected frequencies applies.

## Step-by-step procedure

### 1 × *N* Chi square (test of goodness of fit)

Use this test for *frequency data* only, i.e. for *counts* of different types of 'events'

**Step 1** Draw up the 1 × *N* table, making sure that each event goes into one of the cells and into not more than one cell. The number in each cell is the **observed frequency** $O$ for that cell

**Step 2** Find the **total frequency**

**Step 3** Work out the **expected frequency** $E$ for each cell separately, using the theoretical distribution to be fitted. For the special case of the rectangular distribution we are considering, there is an equal probability of occurrence of the different alternatives.

$$E = \frac{\text{total frequency}}{N} \text{ for each cell}$$

## Worked example

### 1 × N Chi square (test of goodness of fit)

A sample of 250 people in the street were asked to 'say any number from 0 to 9 inclusive'. Do the results show any evidence for number preference?

| Step 1 | Digit | Observed frequency |
|---|---|---|
| | 0 | 18 |
| | 1 | 31 |
| | 2 | 29 |
| | 3 | 36 |
| | 4 | 17 |
| | 5 | 20 |
| | 6 | 20 |
| | 7 | 35 |
| | 8 | 14 |
| | 9 | 30 |

**Step 2** Total frequency = 250

**Step 3** In the absence of number preference, all observed frequencies will have the same expected value

i.e. $E = \dfrac{250}{10} = 25$

## Step-by-step procedure – continued

### 1 × *N* Chi square (test of goodness of fit)

**Step 4** Work out $(O - E)$ for each cell
NB for the 1 d.f. case, Yates's correction must be applied, i.e. take $(|O - E| - \frac{1}{2})$ for each cell

**Step 5** Square this for each cell

**Step 6** Divide by $E$

**Step 7** Obtain $\chi^2$ by adding all these contributions from the different cells

**Step 8** Obtain the degrees of freedom = (number of cells − 1)

**Step 9** If the $\chi^2$ obtained exceeds the value found in Table G at the chosen level of significance, then there is evidence for a divergence between the theoretical and observed distributions

**Step 10** Translate the result of the test back in terms of the experiment

**Worked example – continued**

## $1 \times N$ Chi square (test of goodness of fit)

| $O$ | $E$ | Step 4 $(O - E)$ | Step 5 $(O - E)^2$ | Step 6 $(O - E)^2/E$ |
|-----|-----|------------------|--------------------|----------------------|
| 18 | 25 | $-7$ | 49 | 1·96 |
| 31 | 25 | 6 | 36 | 1·44 |
| 29 | 25 | 4 | 16 | 0·64 |
| 36 | 25 | 11 | 121 | 4·84 |
| 17 | 25 | $-8$ | 64 | 2·56 |
| 20 | 25 | $-5$ | 25 | 1·00 |
| 20 | 25 | $-5$ | 25 | 1·00 |
| 35 | 25 | 10 | 100 | 4·00 |
| 14 | 25 | $-11$ | 121 | 4·84 |
| 30 | 25 | 5 | 25 | 1·00 |

**Step 7**
$$\chi^2 = \Sigma\frac{(O - E)^2}{E} = 1·96 + 1·44 + 0·64 + 4·84 +$$
$$+ 2·56 + 1·00 + 1·00 + 4·00 +$$
$$+ 4·84 + 1·00$$
$$= 23·28$$

**Step 8** d.f. = (number of cells $-$ 1) = 9

**Step 9** From Table G, $\chi^2 = 16·92$ at the 5 per cent significance level with 9 d.f. As the observed $\chi^2$ exceeds the table $\chi^2$ at the 5 per cent level, there is evidence for a significant departure from equal choices of the different digits

**Step 10** The results of the experiment show significant evidence for number preferences

# 7 Parametric and non-parametric tests

## Parametric tests

As discussed in Chapter 5, the $t$-test and the variance-ratio test make certain assumptions about the underlying population distributions of the data on which they are used; for example that they are normal. Such tests are often called 'parametric' as these assumptions are about population parameters. (*Parameters* are measures computed from all the observations in a population – examples are the population mean and standard deviation. *Statistics* are measures computed from a sample, in order to estimate parameters.)

Parametric tests are often *robust*, in that they are relatively unaffected by violations of these assumptions (see p. 75). But some situations arise where there are markedly non-normal distributions, or where the data collected are in the form of rankings (first, second, etc.) rather than the scores.

A range of tests, commonly referred to as *non-parametric* (or *rank order*) tests, have been developed which can be used in these situations. They can also be used where it would be appropriate to use parametric tests (while you can't convert a rank into a score, scores can be turned into ranks). In fact some enthusiasts for non-parametric tests urge their virtually universal use, but there are some disadvantages which are discussed below (p. 122).

## The Mann-Whitney and Wilcoxon tests

The Mann-Whitney and Wilcoxon tests are two non-parametric tests, which do a very similar job to the independent samples and correlated samples $t$-tests respectively. While their use means that you can have a more relaxed approach to the type of data to be analysed it is worth stressing that an experiment which is to be analysed using a non-parametric test needs just as careful attention to points of experimental design, randomization, etc., as one to be analysed using a parametric test.

These tests are based on orderings or rankings of the data. Suppose that a person is asked to rank in order of preference eight foods, four of which are savoury and four sweet. If they rank the four sweet foods as first, second, third and fourth, then it would appear likely that they prefer sweet foods to savoury foods. The mathematical basis for this is straightforward. If we had the names of the foods written on cards and shuffled thoroughly then what would be the chances that the four 'sweet' cards would be turned over first? This probability can be calculated quite simply and is pretty low. Randomization of all possible orderings forms the basis of the Mann-Whitney and Wilcoxon tests. The data can be in the form of rankings, as discussed above, or actual measures can be taken which are then converted into ranks.

A non-parametric test does not usually test exactly the same thing as the corresponding parametric test. Effectively, the general procedure is the same as in the food example just considered. We start with the null hypothesis that each of the orders in which the set of eight cards might be turned over is equally likely to occur. If the IV has no effect on the DV, this will be the case. Then, as in other tests, if the results obtained in an actual experiment are highly improbable given that the above hypothesis is true, we come to the decision that the IV does affect the DV. Another way of putting the distinction between what the parametric and non-parametric tests actually test is to say that, whereas the $t$-test tests for a specific difference in the means of the population, the corresponding non-parametric test is a general test of whether or not the populations are the same.

In general, non-parametric tests tend to be less sensitive at detecting an effect of the independent variable on the dependent variable. Another way of saying this is that in situations where both types of test are appropriate, the **power efficiency** of the non-parametric test is lower than its parametric counterpart. To detect any given effect at a specified significance level, a larger sample size is required for the non-parametric test than the parametric test. This is expressed as

power efficiency of test A compared with test B $= \dfrac{N_B}{N_A} \times 100$,

where $N_A$ is the sample size needed to show a statistically significant effect at the 5 per cent level for test A, and $N_B$ is the sample size needed to show a statistically significant effect at the 5 per cent level for test B.

## Mann-Whitney test

This is the non-parametric counterpart of the independent samples $t$-test for equality of means. Hence, it is appropriate for use with independent-samples designs. It is based on a statistic $U$ which is linked to the sum of the ranks of each of the conditions.

A step-by-step procedure and worked example are given for use with the small-sample case. Table H is used in connection with this and covers situations where the samples have twenty or fewer cases (if the samples are unequal in size, as is possible, of course, with the independent samples design, then the larger of the samples should be twenty or fewer).

## Step-by-step procedure

### Mann-Whitney test – small-sample* case

For **independent samples designs:** use instead of uncorrelated $t$-test if data is either (a) in the form of ranks or (b) obviously non-normal or (c) there is an obvious difference in the variance of the two groups

**Step 1** Rank data (taking both groups together) giving rank 1 to the lowest score, and so on

**Step 2** Find the sum of the ranks for the smaller sample – A in the example opposite – (if both samples are the same size, find the sum of ranks of sample A). Call this $T$

**Step 3** Find $U = N_A N_B + \dfrac{N_A(N_A + 1)}{2} - T$,

where $N_A$ is the number of scores in the smaller sample (or, if both samples are the same size, the sample whose ranks were totalled to find $T$)

**Step 4** Find $U' = N_A N_B - U$

**Step 5** Look up the *smaller* of $U$ and $U'$ in Table H. There is a significant difference if the observed value is equal to or less than the table value

**Step 6** Translate the result of the test back in terms of the experiment

---

## Treatment of ties

Give the mean rank to the tied observations. Thus, if 2 scores of 10 tie for 5th and 6th ranks, give each score a rank of 5·5. If 3 scores of 18 tie for 12th, 13th and 14th ranks, give each score a rank of 13. The test should not be used if there is a large proportion of ties.

* Not more than 20 observations in either set of scores

## Worked example

## Mann-Whitney test – small-sample case

Solution times of anagrams under condition A (single category) or condition B (multiple categories) were as follows:

| A | B | Step 1 | A | B |
|---|---|--------|---|---|
| 3 | 23 | | 1 | 5 |
| 5 | 37 | | 2 | 7 |
| 97 | 64 | | 9 | 8 |
| 12 | 24 | | 3 | 6 |
| | 14 | | | 4 |

**Step 2** $T = 1 + 2 + 9 + 3 = 15$

**Step 3** $N_A = 4, \qquad N_B = 5$

$$U = (4 \times 5) + \frac{(4 \times 5)}{2} - 15$$

$$= 15$$

**Step 4** $U' = (4 \times 5) - U$
$$= 20 - 15$$
$$= 5$$

**Step 5** As $U'$ is less than $U$, look up $U'$ in Table H. Table value for $N_A = 4$, $N_B = 5$ is 1. The observed value (5) is not equal to or less than the table value, therefore there is not significant evidence that the scores under the two conditions differ

**Step 6** Anagram solution times under the two conditions (single and multiple categories) do not differ significantly

## Mann-Whitney test – large-sample test

The sampling distribution of the statistic $U$ approaches the normal distribution when the sample size becomes large. The procedure is to obtain $U$ as in the small-sample case (steps 1–3 inclusive). The standard deviation of $U$ can then be found as

$$SD_U = \sqrt{\frac{N_A N_B (N_A + N_B + 1)}{12}}$$

and a $z$-score (see p. 54) as

$$z = \left( U - \frac{N_A N_B}{2} \right) \div SD_U.$$

If we are dealing with a two-tailed test, then the observed $z$ is significant at the 5 per cent level if it exceeds 1·96. For a one-tailed test, 5 per cent significance is attained if $z$ exceeds 1·64 (check these in Table D if you are in doubt).

The ranking procedure can become quite laborious with large samples. Partly for this reason and partly because violations of the assumptions behind parametric statistics become less important for large samples, the Mann-Whitney test tends to be restricted to use with relatively small samples.

## The Wilcoxon test

This is the non-parametric counterpart to the correlated samples $t$-test for equality of means. It is suitable for use with the matched pairs or repeated measures designs. We have already considered a non-parametric test which is appropriate for use in this design (the sign test, p. 35).

The Wilcoxon test is intermediate between the sign test and the correlated samples $t$-test in the amount of information which is extracted from the data. In the sign test we only take into account the sign of the difference between a pair of scores; in the $t$-test the actual size of the difference is used in computation. The Wilcoxon test uses the sign of the difference and additionally *orders* the sizes of these differences.

As one might expect, the sign test is low in power efficiency (what is power efficiency? See p. 113), the Wilcoxon test intermediate and the correlated samples $t$-test most efficient. However, there is in fact only a small difference in the power efficiencies of Wilcoxon and correlated samples $t$-tests in situations where either could be used.

The Wilcoxon test is similar both in rationale and in computation to the Mann-Whitney test. It is based on a statistic $T$, derived from the sum of the ranks for the differences in the data pairs in the less frequent direction. The step by step procedure and worked example for small samples (taken as twenty-five pairs or fewer) give full details.

## Step-by-step procedure

### Wilcoxon test – small-sample* case

For matched pairs or repeated measures designs: use instead of
a correlated $t$-test if either (a) the differences between treatments
can only be ranked in size or (b) the data is obviously non-normal
or (c) there is an obvious difference in the variance of the two
groups

**Step 1**  Obtain the difference between each pair of readings, taking
sign into account

**Step 2**  Rank order these differences (ignoring the sign), giving
rank 1 to the smallest difference

**Step 3**  Obtain $T$, the sum of the ranks for differences with the less
frequent sign

**Step 4**  Consult Table J. If the observed $T$ is equal to or less than
the table value, then there is a significant difference between
the two conditions

**Step 4**  Translate the result of the test back in terms of the
experiment

* Not more than 25 pairs of scores

## Worked example

### Wilcoxon – small-sample case

Eight pairs of twins were tested in complex reaction time situations; one member of each pair was tested after drinking 3 double whiskies, the other member was completely sober. The following reaction times were recorded:

| Sober group | Whisky group | **Step 1** Differences | **Step 2** Ranks |
|---|---|---|---|
| 310 | 300 | −10 | 1 |
| 340 | 320 | −20 | 2 |
| 290 | 360 | 70 | 5 |
| 270 | 320 | 50 | 4 |
| 370 | 540 | 170 | 6 |
| 330 | 360 | 30 | 3 |
| 320 | 680 | 360 | 7 |
| 320 | 1120 | 800 | 8 |

**Step 3** Less frequent sign of difference is negative,
$T = 1 + 2 = 3$

**Step 4** From Table J, when $N = 8$, $T = 4$. As the observed value of $T$ is less than the table value, there is a significant difference between the two conditions

**Step 5** Complex reaction time scores are significantly higher after drinking 3 double whiskies than when sober

## Wilcoxon test – large-sample case

As with the Mann-Whitney test, the sampling distribution of the statistic (in this case $T$) approaches the normal distribution as the sample size becomes large. Having obtained $T$ as in the small-sample (Steps 1–3 inclusive), the standard deviation of $T$ is found as

$$SD_T = \sqrt{\frac{N(N + 1)(2N + 1)}{24}}$$

and a $z$-score as

$$z = \left\{ T - \frac{N(N + 1)}{4} \right\} \div SD_T.$$

The significance decisions are identical to those for the Mann-Whitney large-sample case. Thus, if we have a two-tailed test, the observed $z$ is significant at the 5 per cent level if it exceeds 1·96. For the one-tailed test, significance is attained if $z$ exceeds 1·64. However, as with the Mann-Whitney test, and for the same reasons, the Wilcoxon test tends to be restricted to use with relatively small samples.

## Comparison of Mann-Whitney and Wilcoxon with $t$-test

The power efficiency of the Mann-Whitney and Wilcoxon tests, whilst usually somewhat lower than the corresponding $t$-test, compares very favourably with it. The Mann-Whitney and Wilcoxon tests can be used in situations where the $t$-test would be inappropriate (e.g. where the assumptions of the $t$-test obviously do not apply). In other words, they are capable of wider application.

Different statisticians give different advice as to the relative merits of parametric and non-parametric tests. The non-parametric camp claim that their tests are simpler to compute, have fewer assumptions and can be used more widely. The parametric camp claim that their tests are robust with respect to violations of their assumptions and have greater power efficiency.

The strategy recommended here is to use the $t$-test *unless* the data is in the form of ranks, *or* where the sample is small, and either the distribution is obviously non-normal or there are obviously large differences in variance.

However, if you are particularly pressed for time or have a large number of analyses to do there is nothing particularly wicked nor inappropriate about using non-parametric statistics, even in cases where *t*-tests might have been used.

# 8 Interrelationship of design and analysis

In Chapter 2 we went through an example which illustrated the steps which have to be taken in designing an experiment. To recap, these were as follows:

Given that you have a problem, a relatively fuzzy idea of the area in which you want to carry out the experiment, the first step is to develop one or more precise **research questions**. These have then to be turned into a form which is capable of being tested experimentally. This means deciding on the **independent variable** and **dependent variable**, and, conventionally, setting up a **null hypothesis** and **alternative hypothesis** in terms of the specific IV and DV. Each of the variables has to be **operationalized**, i.e. you have to state what precisely you do in order to manipulate or measure it. You have also to decide how many levels of the independent variable you are going to use (i.e. how many experimental conditions or treatments). Remember that the techniques presented in this book deal directly only with the comparison of two treatments.

The next decision concerns how participants fit into the experiment. This gives us our three basic experimental designs – **independent samples**, **matched pairs** and **repeated measures**. Then you must decide on how many participants, which will obviously be influenced by many things: how difficult they are to get, how long you can spend with each, and so on. The kind of problem that you start with, coupled with the experimental design, and the type of data that this generates (scores, frequencies or counts, or ranks) effectively decides for you the statistical test (or tests – often more than one would be feasible) which you use. Relying solely on the techniques that are described in this book, there is a good range of experimental designs whose results you can analyse statistically. Of course, there are many designs for which you have not been given the appropriate statistical techniques.

A basic principle is that you should never conduct an experiment without having thought through the ways in which it can be analysed. *The decisions about the statistics to be used must be made as a part of the design process.* If you don't do this you run the grave risk of having data that is unanalysable.

This is always true, no matter how sophisticated an arsenal of statistical techniques is at your disposal. It is only in cases where experimenters have supreme confidence that they can demonstrate the effects of the independent variable completely unequivocally (as happens for instance in some cases with the application of Skinnerian techniques) that statistical analysis may be unnecessary.

## How to increase the sensitivity of an experiment

Many new experimenters get very discouraged by a string of non-significant results. Somebody new to the game is likely to be unskilled in selecting problems amenable to attack by experimentation. An experiment is a precision tool where we are effectively making what might be a very risky bet that a particular independent variable, operationalized in a specific way, has an effect on a particular dependent variable, also operationalized in a specific way. Confidence that you are doing something sensible comes from your building on the work of others (which generally means that you have a good knowledge of the research literature in a particular field), or where you have built up your own knowledge and experience through working in the area.

However, there are a number of general areas to which you can give attention which will help to make your experiments more sensitive at detecting experimental effects.

## 1 Reduce the 'noise' level

By this, I do not mean just the physical sound level. 'Noise' is used figuratively here as a general term to cover the effects of uncontrolled variables. These effects appear in many ways, for instance in the instructions given to participants. If instructions vary slightly from participant to participant, then the scores obtained by participants might vary according to these instructions. If there is poor experimental control over the general conditions in the laboratory, or wherever the experiment takes place (e.g. people talking or laughing, to which the participants may sometimes pay attention and sometimes not), if they are bored with the experiment or more interested in interacting with the experimenter than with the experiment – these can all have effects on the data which have nothing to do with the experimental variable being manipulated.

Standardization and control can be taken too far. There is a good case for our being concerned with experimental effects which are sufficiently strong to show themselves in relatively naturalistic situations. However, if we have decided to follow the experimental approach then the line must be drawn at a point where the 'noise' is at a level where the experimental effects have a chance to come through.

So lesson one is that the sensitivity of an experiment can be increased by increasing the degree of experimental control over the conditions under which the experiment takes place. Given that we have refined our procedures as much as possible, what else can be done?

## 2 More participants

A second possibility is to increase the *sample size* – that is, the number of participants taking part in the experiment. This tends to make the experiment more sensitive because the effect of the experimental variable (assuming that there is an effect) will add together over participants, whereas the random error effects (which we will never be able to get rid of completely) will tend to cancel each other out as some will be in one direction, some in the other.

Another way of saying the same thing is that we are more likely to get a statistically significant result if we increase the sample size. In fact, if statistical significance were all that one was interested in you could virtually guarantee it in *any* experiment by choosing a sufficiently large sample size! This is because there will almost always be some (even though very minor) effect of the IV on the DV. So, somewhat paradoxically, there is a case for paying more attention to statistically significant results obtained from relatively small samples than from those with large samples. The former are more likely to be 'significant' in the sense of 'important' or 'strong' as they have, as it were, emerged successfully from a considerable amount of 'noise' from random effects.

However, in the small experiments that you are likely to be carrying out as novice experimenters, a good rule is to work with as many participants as you can get hold of and deal with properly in the time available.

## 3 Floor and ceiling effects

*Avoid possible 'floor' and 'ceiling' effects* on the measures that you are taking. The level of difficulty of the experimental situation should be adjusted so that scores lie in the mid-range of any scale that is used. If, in a memory experiment, all the participants score between 90 and 100 per cent correct, with a lot of 100s, then any difference between experimental conditions would be reduced simply because the results of some participants are bumping on the ceiling and hence not going as high as they would otherwise. The converse occurs if the material is too difficult and floor effects result.

The solution lies in careful pilot work to establish the kind of scores participants are likely to obtain *under the precise conditions of the experiment.*

## 4 Increasing reliability of the measure

Another way in which the sensitivity can be increased is by *increasing the reliability of the measures to be analysed.* One way in which this can be done in psychological experimentation is by basing the measure not on a single observation but on a series of observations and then using the mean or some other measure of central tendency in analysis. Any random effect unconnected with the experimental effect, say due to a loud noise just before an observation is made, might influence a single observation a great deal, but would have much less effect on the median score. Consider carefully, of course, whether the experiment is such that taking a series of observations from a single participant is possible. In doing that, we are assuming that the observations are independent of each other, that they are all measures of the same thing. The reasonableness of this assumption varies very much from one experimental situation to another.

## 5 Which design?

Finally, one should consider the relative sensitivity of the independent samples, matched pairs and repeated measures designs. Generally, the sensitivity increases as one goes from independent samples to matched pairs to repeated measures. This is due to the increasing degree of control over any variables associated with participants. In a repeated measures design it is the same participant who appears under both conditions. In so far as scores under the experimental conditions may be affected by such things as age, sex, intelligence, personality characteristics, etc., we obviously have perfect matching, and hence direct control over these variables, when it is the same participant under both conditions.

With the matched pairs design we retain some matching, but this is usually done on just a single variable. Hence the degree of matching is less than with repeated measures and the efficiency of the design will depend on how close a correlation exists between the matching variable and the dependent variable. If there is a high correlation, then the matching will be very effective. Your problem is to find variables with this high degree of correlation. It is not easy.

With independent samples designs there is no attempt at all to match participants on a one-to-one basis, and therefore no participant variables are controlled, and this design is the least sensitive.

This analysis should not be taken as an indication that we always aim for repeated measures designs and avoid independent samples designs. The great weakness of repeated measures designs lies simply in the fact that they have repeated measures! Because participants have to perform under both experimental conditions, there are all kinds of nasty effects which might occur.

One of the special features of humans is the extent to which they are learning animals: the extent to which their present behaviour is modified by their past experiences. If we test the same person under two conditions there is likely to be an order effect. The result of the second test may well be modified by their experience on the first one. Counterbalancing or randomization of the order of presentation of the two conditions can and should be used, but it will only completely neutralize a simple order effect which adds (or subtracts) a constant amount to, or from, whatever is done second. There is no guarantee that the effects will be as simple as this.

Because of this the repeated measures design is best used in situations where the order effect is known to be small or negligible – for example in simple motor tasks where no knowledge of results is provided to participants. Alternatively, if the random variability between participants on a dependent variable was very high (so that an independent samples design would be unlikely to yield any results), one might be tempted to use a repeated measures design.

It is possible to convert an independent samples design into a matched pairs design, providing that some meaningful way of matching can be devised (i.e. a matching variable which is known to correlate reasonably highly with performance on the dependent variable). The only disadvantage is the labour involved in getting the scores on the matching variable to make up the pairs of participants.

The strategy suggested then is to use a matched pairs design if there is a matching variable which correlates highly with the dependent variable. If this is not available, then a choice between independent samples and repeated measures designs depends upon the likelihood that repeated measures would be independent. If this appears unlikely, the independent samples design should be used.

## More complex designs

Some indications of the kinds of ways in which the basic experimental designs can be complicated will now be considered.

### More than two experimental conditions

Whilst it is possible to use our two-condition experimental design in order to test for the effect of the independent variable, there are several defects to this simple design. It may happen, for instance, that the two values of the independent variable which we have chosen happen not to show any effects, whereas the choice of two other values might have shown an effect. The obvious way of getting over this difficulty is to include a larger number of experimental conditions and to look for differences between these conditions.

You can use the *t*-test (or its non-parametric equivalents where appropriate) to look at conditions in pairs, but there are difficulties connected with significance level if this is done. Do not forget that a 5 per cent significance level means that there is a 5 per cent chance of mistakenly deciding that the IV is affecting the DV when only random effects are present. This means that if you made 20 comparisons between pairs of conditions, you would expect 1 of these 20 (i.e. 5 out of 100, or 5 per cent) to come up with a significant effect *even when there is no actual effect of IV on DV*. Similarly, if you just look at the results after they have been obtained, and pick out, say, the conditions with lowest and highest means, you are effectively going through all the other tests implicitly and the difficulties with significance level remain even though one might only compute a single *t*-test.

A second criticism of experiments with only two experimental conditions is that, whereas they can indicate whether or not an independent variable has an effect on a dependent variable (if we are lucky or cunning with the particular levels of the IV that we have chosen), they cannot tell us anything of the nature or the relationship between the two variables.

Figure 24 shows three different possibilities which would fit in

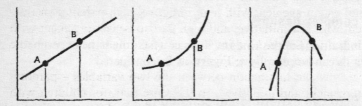

Figure 24　Three different relationships between independent and dependent variables consistent with known values at A and B

with the same results on conditions A and B. The only way in which the nature of these relationships can be made clear is by including in the same experiment several values on the independent variable, so that more points can be filled in on the graph.

A statistical technique which is useful for designs with several levels of the independent variable is the **analysis of variance**, which is covered in detail in most advanced texts of psychological statistics.

## More than one independent variable

There is no reason why an experimental design need be limited to a single independent variable. The design can be extended to include as many variables as you wish but there are considerable advantages over single independent variable experiments if just two IVs are included.

One such design involves all possible combinations of levels of the different IVs, and is known as a **factorial design**. It can tell us about the effect of a particular IV, not just when all other variables are held constant (as in the single variable design), but over the different levels of the other IV.

A great advantage of factorial designs is that they bring out possible **interactions** between variables. An interaction occurs when the effect of one independent variable is not constant, but varies according to the level of another independent variable.

Suppose, for example, that a number of children were assessed on their degree of initiative on the one hand, and the extent of parental encouragement on the other. Four groups of children were formed: low parental encouragement with low initiative, low parental encouragement with high initiative, high parental encouragement with low initiative, and high parental encouragement with high initiative. Subsequent intelligence tests might have given the results shown graphically in Figure 25.

This shows an interaction between the two variables – parental encouragement and initiative – in the sense that, for children with low parental encouragement it made little or no difference whether they had low or high initiative. For children with high parental encouragement, those with high initiative scored considerably higher than those with low initiative.

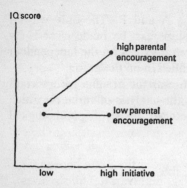

Figure 25  Interaction between the variables of parental encouragement and initiative

These (fictitious) results can also be used to repeat earlier warnings about the interpretation of the findings in a study. It is highly unlikely that a study of this type was an experiment involving random assignment of participants to the different parental encouragement and initiative conditions. So, any inferences about causative relationships are very difficult to make because of the possible existence of other factors.

Designs involving more than one independent variable cannot be analysed directly by the techniques covered in this text. The analysis of variance, referred to in the previous section, would commonly be used. It would be possible to perform separate analyses of the effect of parental encouragement on low-initiative children (e.g. a $t$-test in each case). Alternatively, or additionally, one could perform a similar test on the effect of initiative on the group with low parental encouragement and then the effect of initiative on the group with high parental encouragement.

Such tests can provide some kind of analysis of the data, but do not tell us anything directly about possible interactions, and they are really not an adequate substitute for a full analysis.

## More than one dependent variable

Just as it is possible to make use of more than one independent variable, so you can have more than one dependent variable. There might be advantages in looking at the effect of a particular independent variable on several dependent variables. If, for example, we are investigating the effects of sleep deprivation, it might appear sensible to use a battery of different testing situations, some cognitive, some perceptual, and so on.

If it is necessary to find the effects of more than one dependent variable simultaneously, then so-called 'multivariate' procedures should be used. Most of these procedures are extremely complicated and tedious to compute and it would be foolish to adopt them without appropriate computer software which can do the drudgery for you. However, designs using a single dependent variable can be applied appropriately to many research problems. In practice it is often impossible to measure more than two or three dependent variables. These can be used one by one in separate analyses, although, as with multiple independent variables, important aspects might be lost by doing this.

# 9 Carrying out the experiment and writing it up

## Carrying out the experiment

Once you have designed your experiment, the next stage involves actually getting to grips with your participants, as it were. The essential thing here is that you know exactly what you are going to do before you attempt to do it. There are a number of things that will help you to do this.

(1) Have verbatim (word-for-word) instructions for your participants.

(2) Have a prepared work sheet which shows you clearly what you have to do and the order in which you have to do it. It should also have spaces into which you can fit the results as you get them. Figure 26 shows an example of a work sheet.

(3) If you have apparatus, make sure it works and that you know what to do with it to perform appropriately.

(4) If this is a laboratory-type experiment, make sure that your participant is adequately screened from (a) your experimenter, together with your work sheet and any other information which should not be available to the participant, (b) other participants and experimenters and the world at large. Obviously, sound-proofed cubicles are a great help in many experimental situations, but common sense can remove a lot of the possible interference and distraction from your participants, e.g. using visual presentation of material and a visual metro-

| _Orientation_ A | | | | | | | | _Orientation_ B | | | | | | | |
| comparison stimulus | | | | | | | | comparison stimulus | | | | | | | |
| 1 | 2 | 3 | 4 | 5 | 6 | 7 | 8 | 1 | 2 | 3 | 4 | 5 | 6 | 7 | 8 |
|---|---|---|---|---|---|---|---|---|---|---|---|---|---|---|---|
| 11 +| 3 +| 5 +| 8 −| 1 +| 13 −| 2 −| 6 −| 9 +| 1 +| 2 −| 6 −| 4 −| 7 −| 14 | 3 −|
| 16 +| 4 +| 12 +| 10 +| 9 −| 14 −| 7 −| 15 −| 10 +| 5 −| 12 | 11 | 15 | 13 | 16 | 8 −|
|  |  |  |  |  |  |  |  |  |  |  |  |  |  |  |  |
|  |  |  |  |  |  |  |  |  |  |  |  |  |  |  |  |
|  |  |  |  |  |  |  |  |  |  |  |  |  |  |  |  |
|  |  |  |  |  |  |  |  |  |  |  |  |  |  |  |  |
|  |  |  |  |  |  |  |  |  |  |  |  |  |  |  |  |

Figure 26  An example of a worksheet.
Sixteen trials have been presented under orientation A, the randomized order of presentation being indicated by the numbers in the cell. These are followed by 16 trials under orientation B, 10 of which have been presented – comparison stimulus 4 would be presented next. There would be 64 trials under each condition, counterbalanced according to the sequence ABAB–BABA (in blocks of 16). The 'scores' are simply + or −, indicating a judgement of 'greater than' or 'less than'

nome (light flashing at intervals) for pacing of material or response, rather than using auditory presentation.

(5) **Most important of all, have adequate pilot trials before you start the experiment proper.** This ensures that the instructions are intelligible to the participants and that they can perform appropriately in the situation. It helps you avoid 'floor' or 'ceiling' effects (what are floor and ceiling effects? See p. 127) by

adjusting the difficulty of the material depending on how the pilot participants perform. You will find out as experimenter whether the task you have set yourself is feasible, e.g. whether you have enough time to make the appropriate manipulations and write down the results of one trial before the next is due, and so on. Quite often inexperienced experimenters will set themselves a task as experimenter which is way above the perceptual and/or cognitive capabilities of the human being. From the time taken by the pilot participants, you will be able to work out how long the experiment proper will take and to see whether you have seriously under-budgeted (likely) or over-budgeted (unlikely) on this.

After you have, if necessary, modified the procedures in the light of the pilot trials – and done further pilot work if the changes were extensive – then you are ready to go, and the best of luck!

## Experimenter effects

Many studies have shown that, if experimenters have an expectation that the results will turn out in a particular way, then they may influence the results by their expectations. The participant-experimenter situation is a social situation and it may well be that the participant attempts to please the experimenter by performing according to your expectations, wishes or hopes. Cues such as tone of voice, brusqueness or friendliness, sharpness of movement, involuntary noises of pleasure or despair can all influence the results in the desired direction. The answer to all this is to standardize the procedure as much as possible and, if a situation appears to be one where experimenter effects could be serious, to use blind techniques, e.g. with the experimenter handing over the running of the experiment to some other person who does not know the experimenter's expectations or hypothesis. There are many fascinating experiments one could carry out on the experimenter effect itself.

## Care and treatment of participants

Participants are precious things, as you will find out if you want to run an experiment with a large number of participants from a particular population (e.g. male left-handers aged from twenty to thirty years). You must treat them properly. Psychologists are increasingly sensitive to the ethics of experimentation and the British Psychological Society has a 'Code of Conduct' covering this, and other areas of the work of psychologists (BPS, 1993) which you should refer to. Similar codes have been developed by the American Psychological Association and other national bodies.

The essential principle is that the experiment, or other investigation, should be considerd from the standpoint of all participants. Foreseeable threats to their psychological well-being, health, values or dignity should be eliminated. Important aspects of this are:

### Consent

Participants should give their *informed consent*. The involves telling them in as much detail as possible what it is they will be asked to do and how long it will take. Remember also that many participants will be rather apprehensive and nervous in the experimental situation and that it is in your interest to get them calm and happy before you start.

### Deception

Withholding information or misleading participants is unacceptable if they are likely to object or show unease when told about the real nature of the experiment. If it is essential for the purposes of the experiment that participants should be misled as to what it is all about, this should only be done under the supervision of an experienced experimental psychologist, and with the approval of an 'ethics committee' or other appropriate group.

### Debriefing

Participants must be put fully in the picture as soon as possible after the experiment. Discussing with them their experience of the experiment can not only help you monitor any unforeseen negative effects or misconceptions, but often provides interesting insights which help in its interpretation.

It is also courteous to let your participants know what your findings were, after you have analysed the results. People are often fascinated by the results of experiments in which they were involved and it is in your own interest, if you want to do further experiments, to keep their interest well-stoked.

## Withdrawal from the experiment

Participants should know from the outset that they have the right to withdraw *at any time*. This can make things difficult for you as an experimenter, but it certainly encourages you to ensure that it will be an experience from which they won't want to withdraw.

## Confidentiality

Participants have a right to expect that any information they provide about themselves in the experimental situation will be treated confidentially and if published in any way (including your experimental reports) it will not be identifiable as theirs. If, for any reason, this is not the case then they should know this before consenting to take part.

## Writing up the experiment

Having carried out the experiment, you have next to analyse the results using those statistical techniques which you have previously decided would answer the questions that you are interested in, and which are appropriate to the experimental design and the kind of data collected.

It might appear that, having analysed and interpreted the results, that is the end of it. But, no – if you performed a worthwhile experiment then others ought to know about it. Which brings us to the experimental report. Whether one is dealing with the first faltering experimental effort of the student, or the thousandth publication of the Nobel prizewinner, the objects of the exercise are the same: to inform the reader about the findings and how they were obtained, and to explain their relevance. In other words, how do the results fit in with previous data and/or theories, or with the theory presented in the report?

## Suggested sub-headings for an experimental report

There is no one correct way of presenting an experimental report. However, the use of standardized sub-headings does help to provide a check-list to ensure that nothing important has been omitted. The following set of sub-headings is put forward in that spirit.

### 1 Title

This can often be given simply in terms of the independent variable and dependent variable, e.g. 'To investigate the effect of word frequency on recognition' or 'The effect of overtraining on discrimination reversal'.

### 2 Introduction

This begins with a general statement of the problem. It continues with a review of previous experimental work in the area (with references) and the explanations or theories which have been associated with the previous work. It then leads on to a statement of the hypothesis or hypotheses to be investigated. Some prefer to have the hypothesis as a separate section, others have it as a subsection of the introduction.

### 3 Method

In this section the reader is told exactly what was done in the experiment. The best way of deciding what should fit in this section is by asking the question – could the reader repeat the experiment exactly using the information given? It is useful to subdivide this section as follows:

## a Design

A succinct statement of the variables in the experiment, together with their operational definition. The type of design (independent samples, matched samples or repeated measures) should be given together with an indication of how participants are assigned to conditions and how other variables are controlled.

## b Participants

State the type and number of participants and give a brief description of the population from which they are drawn, together with the procedures used for obtaining the experimental sample. (In some cases you may be unable to sample, e.g. when the participants are drawn from your own class or group – if this is the case, say so.)

## c Apparatus and materials

Any apparatus used should be described in sufficient detail for a reader to obtain the same. If the apparatus is available commercially, the manufacturer's name and the type or model number should be given. If it is not commercially available then details of construction and dimensions should be given. A fully labelled diagram is often very helpful.

Any materials specially prepared should be described here (e.g. sheets on which responses are to be made; jumbled words or anagrams). It may help to include an example in an appendix.

## d Procedure

This consists of a detailed step-by-step description of exactly what happened when the experiment was taking place. It should include all the things that happened to participants between their coming into the room and leaving it. Verbatim (word for word) instructions should be given whenever possible. The way in which stimuli are presented to the participant should be detailed, together with the way in which the response is made (verbal, written, etc.). Any time intervals or limits imposed by the experimenter should be given (e.g. participant given a maximum of two minutes to recall the items; rate of presentation of slides was one per five seconds).

## 4 Results

The results should be presented as simply and clearly as possible. Make use of tables and of graphs, histograms or scattergrams. If, as is often the case, the analysis is concerned with the mean scores under two conditions, display these means very clearly. All too often such scores are tucked away almost out of sight. Any graphs should be understandable in their own right without reference back to the text, so they should be fully labelled on both axes, showing the units of measurement where appropriate. Remember that the convention is that the independent variable appears on the horizontal axis, the dependent variable on the vertical axis.

As well as the display and description of your results, this section should include the results of the statistical tests performed. An essential part of this is the statistical significance level associated with the results of the analysis. A common fault of new experimenters is to quote the significance of the result and stop short at that – 'this result is significant at the 5 per cent level'. Remember that you are not doing the statistical analysis just for its own sake. You are doing it for the light it throws on your experiment. So you must go on from this statement of significance to explain what this means in terms of the experiment – 'this result is statistically significant at the 5 per cent level, i.e. the mean time to react in the "alcohol" condition exceeded that in the control condition at the 5 per cent level of significance'.

It is not usually necessary to include all the experimental observations nor the details of the statistical computations in the body of the report. They can, however, be included as a appendix to the experimental report, which has the advantage that anyone going over the report can check details of computation and give help if you are making any mistakes.

## 5 Discussion

The discussion starts with the results of the statistical analysis and their bearing on the hypothesis or hypotheses that were put forward in the introduction. It then goes on to consider their relevance both in theoretical and practical terms. The way in which these results tie in with previous results is considered, together with suggestions for research leading out of the present work.

Limitations of the usefulness of the results should be considered here. It may be, for instance, that certain variables were, avoidably or unavoidably, left uncontrolled. The effect of this lack of control should be considered carefully. Be realistic about this. You cannot expect to control everything and just because, say, the wind changed direction in the middle of the experiment it doesn't necessarily mean that you throw up your hands in despair and the whole experiment is worthless. There may, of course, be occasions when the lack of control of one or more variables does mean that the experiment is inconclusive. All that one can do here is to recommend that the experiment be re-run with appropriate changes. Even an experiment of this type is not a complete waste of time; it has at least made a contribution towards your education as an experimenter.

## References

A common convention is to indicate all references in the body of the write-up by a name and date, e.g. 'As Clark and Stephenson (1989) and Ellis et al. (1993) have pointed out . . .'

The reference section of the experimental write-up puts all the references together in alphabetical order of the authors' names. Thus your reference section might read (in part):

Clark, N. K. and Stephenson, G. M. (1989) 'Group remembering', in P. B. Paulus (ed.) *Psychology of Group Influence*, Erlbaum.

Ellis, H. D., Ellis, D. M. and Hosie, J. A. (1993) 'Priming effects in children's face recognition', *British Journal of Psychology*, 84, 101–110.

Webley, P., Robben, H., Elffers, H. and Hessing, D. (1991) *Tax Evasion: an experimental approach*, Cambridge University Press.

For journal articles, as with the Ellis et al. article referred to above, the sequence is author's name, year of publication, title of article, title of journal, volume number, and first and last pages of the article. Note, by the way, that a convention is to use 'et al.' (i.e. 'and others') in the text of your report when three or more authors are involved.

## Some general points about writing up experiments

An experiment should be written up as soon as possible after the experiment itself is completed. This is important both in motivational and informational terms. If you are still 'involved' with the experiment, then the report will not be a chore, but will appear as a necessary completion of the whole process. It is a bad habit to write up experiments in batches. A great deal of information loss and of interference between experiments is possible with this approach. I have seen some fascinating examples of transposition of procedure between the accounts of one experiment and another. However full and clear your notes appear at the time of the experiment, leaving the write-up for a few weeks will often transform them into confusing hieroglyphics.

As far as presentation of reports is concerned, there is a lot in favour of a ring binder, particularly if you are carrying out a set of experiments. In this way material can be readily added or removed, the order of presentation of different reports changed, and so on.

It is also sensible to have a look at some good examples of experimental reports produced by people in similar situations to yourself. Published articles are worth looking at, providing that you are not put off by complex statistics and other features beyond your present capabilities. Have a look through books of readings containing journal articles. Or, if you have access to libraries possessing journals of experimental psychology you could look through some recent copies.

# 10 Conclusion

This book started out with the assumption that you wished to carry out an experiment and had a problem which you wanted to turn into an experiment, but you did not know how to go about it. Well, hopefully, if you have worked through the book, you should now know something of how to go about it. However, one of the things which has not been discussed is where you get hold of the problems or issues to turn into experiments.

## Ideas for experiments

It is not at all difficult to come up with ideas which could form the base for some kind of inquiry. Once you look at the world about you in this light then I would be surprised if you were not inundated with possibilities. Observe the behaviour of other people, of children, of animals, of yourself. Why do I find it difficult to remember the names of people I have just met, whereas my wife remembers everybody's name? Why does the cat make a strange noise on the kitchen windowsill when there is a squirrel or a magpie outside, and not when dogs, cats or other birds are there? It would be possible to work such questions up into an experiment. By careful observation you would pick out regularities and get ideas about what the variables might be. However, unless you are prepared to devote a considerable part of your life to this enterprise it is highly unlikely that you would, unaided, be able to develop worthwhile experiments.

Remember that, in experimentation, we select a very small number of variables, operationalized in a particular way. To get to the stage where you are able to do this sensibly calls for a lot of preparatory investigation. Given time you could do this through exploratory studies (the experiment is not the only kind of study possible; see Robson, 1993 for coverage of other possibilities). However, although psychology is a young science, it does exist and it is foolish to ignore the work that has been done previously by others.

How does one make a start, then? Any general introductory text will give you some ideas of the way in which psychologists have carved up the field. From this, using your references, you should be able to move to more specialized books and on to journal articles. A large proportion of the 'meat' of psychology is in journal articles, and you need access to a library which subscribes to the main psychological journals.

Once you have a clear idea of the particular area you are interested in and some idea of the ways in which experiments in the area have been carried out and the theoretical frameworks in which they have been cast, it is a good strategy to switch the attack to the most recent work in the area. To do this, *Psychological Abstracts* is a valuable journal. If you look over the last two years for your particular topic you should discover several suitable references (one can sift through the abstracts very quickly). Looking up the references – and the references they cite – quickly gives one an idea of the main issues in the area. Academic libraries are now likely to have abstracting journals such as this on CD-ROM (on a compact disk similar to those used for music but which can be 'played' through a microcomputer – and which can store an amazing amount of information). Your library may also have other forms of computer search facilities. These techniques enable the searcher to go back in time – reference is made in articles to something previously published. However, it may well turn out that a search of this kind turns up a reference which is absolutely central to what you are interested in, and it is then very useful to know whether other researchers have followed it up.

This means going forward in time, and publications called *Citation Indices* enable this to be done. Here the index for a given year gives (amongst other things) the authors who, in their own articles, have cited a particular article.

The process is of course not simply one of checking up in the literature to find out if someone has already performed the experiment that you are interested in. As you read about the approaches which researchers have used and the results they have obtained, your own approach will be altered. What we are describing is a continuous interaction between your own changing ideas and the ideas you encounter in your search of the literature. It may well be that, at the end of this process, you decide that the problem does not exist any more – that it is as satisfactorily explained now as it is likely to be for some time. It may be, however, that the experiments which you have read about seem to ignore something which you feel is vital. If so, go ahead and do not be afraid of breaking out of the framework within which people are working in the area. It may be that they are so involved in following a particular line that they 'can't see the wood for the trees'. They could be making unnecessary assumptions which you as a newcomer may well not share.

This kind of 'enquiry driven' approach is an excellent way of learning a great deal of psychology.

## What to do if the techniques covered here cannot be used to answer the questions you are interested in

Do not despise the armoury of tests provided in this book. Very many problems can be attacked by considering the difference between pairs of means ($t$-tests) or of variances (variance-ratio tests). And if the normality and/or homogeneity of variance assumptions of the $t$-test cannot be justified, there are the non-parametric equivalents. Adding in Spearman's rho (or Pearson's r – see Appendix 2) when we are interested in correlation, and chi square where we have frequency data and want to test for association or goodness of fit, there are many more problems which can be tackled.

However, you may find cases where the problem can only be forced into a mould where one of these tests would be appropriate by altering it out of all recognition. This may mean that you will have to curb your impatience until you have a command of statistics which cover more complex designs. There are many second-level texts to help you with this (e.g. Wright and Fowler, 1986, which is keyed into the present text). Do remember, however, that there is no general rule that the design and carrying out of experiments is a solitary activity. There is much to gain in collaborating with others in all the stages in the process. Nor should you be afraid of asking for advice from those more experienced than yourself.

## What do I do next?

You could try doing an experiment. But beware – they can be addictive.

# References

Baddeley, A. (1981), 'The cognitive psychology of everyday life', *British Journal of Psychology*, vol. 72, pp. 257–269.

Barber, T. X. (1976), *Pitfalls in Human Research: ten pivotal points*, Pergamon.

British Psychological Society (1993), *Code of Conduct, Ethical Principles and Guidelines*, BPS (mimeo).

Hayes, W. (1981), *Statistics*, 3rd edn., Holt, Rinehart and Winston.

Robson, C. (1993), *Real World Research: a resource for social scientists and practitioner-researchers*, Blackwell.

Shipman, M. (1988), *The Limitations of Social Research*, 3rd edn., Longman.

Sidman, M. (1960), *Tactics of Scientific Research*, Basic Books.

Siegel, S. and Castellan, N. J. (1988), *Nonparametric Statistics for the Behavioural Sciences*, 2nd edn., McGraw-Hill.

Wright, G. and Fowler, C. (1986), *Investigative Design and Statistics*, Penguin.

# Appendix 1
## Using random number tables

Randomization is necessary at several stages of most experiments. For instance we might want to:

(a) Select a sample of ten participants at random from a population of a hundred.

(b) Allocate five participants to an experimental group, five to a control group.

(c) Randomize the order of presentation of eight stimulus cards separately for each of ten different trials.

(d) Present pairs of random digits.

(e) Prepare fifty all-consonant nonsense syllable trigrams (i.e. letter combinations).

The basic principle in randomization is to ensure that all the possible alternatives have an equal chance of occurring. It is unsatisfactory for experimenters to try to generate random sequences by simply producing the alternatives in what appears to them to be a random order. There are for instance strong number preferences. Random number tables (e.g. Table A, pp. 158–60) are very valuable. They simply consist of a large set of digits (nowadays usually produced by computer) in which 0, 1, 2, 3, 4, 5, 6, 7, 8 and 9 each have the same probability of occurrence at each position in the table. Provided that this basic fact about the table is remembered, it is a matter of common sense to use the table so that it produces the kind of randomization required. One general point is that the table should ideally be entered at a random position ('pseudo-random' is good enough, e.g. stabbing a finger at it whilst looking away) and then movement from the point selected should be randomly up or down, left or right. The point behind this is that, if you always start at the top left-hand corner and went from left to right, then you would end up with the same sequence every time.

## a Selecting a sample of ten participants at random from a population of a hundred

Number the participants in the population from 0 to 99. Enter the random number table in a pseudo-random manner and use pairs of digits. Travelling, say, downwards from the point selected in the table, write down the first 10 pairs of digits you come to. Pick out the participants corresponding to those numbers (NB the first 10 participants in the population are represented by 00, 01, 02, 03, 04, 05, 06, 07, 08 and 09).

## b Allocating five participants to an experimental group, five to a control group

Let the even digits in the random number table represent the experimental group, the odd digits the control group. Again enter the random number table in a pseudo-random manner, but this time use single digits. Travel, say, left to right from the point selected in the table. If the first digit is odd, then the first participant goes in the control group. If it is even, then the first participant goes in the experimental group. Continue in the same way until five participants have been allocated to one of the two groups. The remaining participants go into the other group.

An alternative (simpler) procedure would be to spin a coin for each participant, 'heads' for experimental, 'tails' for control. Again continue until five participants had been allocated to one of the groups and allocate the remainder to the other group.

## c Randomizing the order of presentation of eight stimulus cards separately for each of ten different trials

Number the eight stimulus cards 1 to 8. Use random number tables and enter them in a pseudo-random manner. Travelling, say, right to left from the point selected in the table note down the first occurrence of each of the digits 1 to 8.

To make this clear, suppose that the line chosen from the random number table is

97 08 14 24 01    51 95 46 30 32    3 ③ 19 00 14

Suppose we start at the circled 3 then, moving right to left, the sequence obtained is 3 2 6 4 5 1 8 7. Notice that 0 and 9 are ignored, as are second and subsequent occurrences of the digits 1 to 8. If necessary one would, of course, continue on the next line until the full sequence was obtained.

On trial one, then, stimulus 3 is presented first, then stimulus 2, then stimulus 6, etc. By continuing in the table one can obtain a total of ten different sequences which will decide the order of presentation for each of the ten different trials.

An alternative procedure would be to take the stimulus cards themselves and to shuffle them thoroughly between trials. It is essential to shuffle extremely thoroughly, however (say two minutes of continual shuffling).

## d Presenting pairs of random digits

For this, you simply use the random number tables directly, entering the tables in the normal pseudo-random fashion and taking pairs of digits.

## e Preparing fifty all-consonant nonsense syllable trigrams (i.e. 3-letter combinations)

If you simply want to produce sets of three consonants where the consonants occur purely randomly, then random number tables can be used. One of many ways of doing this would be to code the consonants as follows:

B-00, C-01, D-02, F-03, G-04, H-05, J-06, K-07, L-08, M-09, N-10, P-11, Q-12, R-13, S-14, T-15, V-16, W-17, X-18, Z-19.

(NB Y is considered as a vowel-equivalent and is omitted from this list.) You enter the random number tables as before and, working with pairs of digits, simply note down the occurrence of any of the code numbers.

For example, working left or right along the line:

64 <u>17</u> 47 67 87 59 81 40 72 61 <u>14</u> <u>00</u> 28

The code numbers occurring are 17, 14, 00; hence, decoding, the trigram is WSB.

As you will have noted, a large proportion of the random number table is not used with this method, and a little ingenuity will provide a more efficient method. If, for instance, we were to again use pairs of digits but simply note whether the first digit of a pair is odd or even, then we could use the code

B-odd-0, C-odd-1, D-odd-2, F-odd-3, G-odd-4, H-odd-5, J-odd-6, K-odd-7, L-odd-8, M-odd-9, N-even-0, P-even-1, Q-even-2, R-even-3, S-even-4, T-even-5, V-even-6, W-even-7, X-even-8, Z-even-9.

Then with the same line as before, we can make use of all pairs of digits, e.g. 64, 17, 47 decodes as SKW.

NB There are lists of nonsense syllables in specialized texts which are scaled in various ways, e.g. for association value, meaningfulness, etc.

# Appendix 2
## Pearson's correlation coefficient (r)

The main part of the text covered the correlation coefficient called Spearman's rho. This appendix is devoted to a second correlation coefficient known as **Pearson's r**; or sometimes as **Pearson's product-moment correlation coefficient**. Whereas Spearman's rho is based on rankings, Pearson's r is calculated from the scores themselves. It is somewhat more laborious to compute than Spearman's rho but tends to be preferred by statisticians. It is also the basis for a number of techniques used in more advanced statistics.

The basic idea behind it is very simple. Table 1 shows two sets of scores $X$ and $Y$, with the $X$ scores arranged in decreasing order of size. The table also gives means ($\bar{X}$ and $\bar{Y}$) and, in the third and fourth columns the deviations from these means ($x = (X - \bar{X})$ and $y = (Y - \bar{Y})$) for each $X$ and $Y$ score. The final, fifth column gives

*Table 1* Showing the calculation of cross-products ($xy$)

| $X$ | $Y$ | $x = (X - \bar{X})$ | $y = (Y - \bar{Y})$ | $xy$ |
|-----|-----|---------------------|---------------------|------|
| 19  | 12  | +9                  | +4                  | +36  |
| 14  | 16  | +4                  | +8                  | +32  |
| 10  | 8   | 0                   | 0                   | 0    |
| 7   | 7   | −3                  | −1                  | +3   |
| 6   | 4   | −4                  | −4                  | +16  |
| 4   | 1   | −6                  | −7                  | +42  |

$\Sigma x = 60 \quad \Sigma Y = 48$

$\bar{X} = \dfrac{60}{6} = 10 \quad \bar{Y} = \dfrac{48}{6} = 8$

the product $(x \times y)$ for each pair of deviations. It is these 'cross-products', as they are called, which are the heart of Pearson's r.

Consider, as in the present case, where there is a positive correlation between $X$ and $Y$; that is where high $X$ and high $Y$ scores tend to go together, and where low $X$ and low $Y$ scores tend to go together. High scores will be above the mean and hence produce positive deviations which when multiplied together give positive cross-products ($xy$s). But the low scores tend to produce negative $X$ and negative $Y$ deviations which when multiplied together also produce positive cross-products. So, for a positive correlation the sum of the cross-products ($\Sigma xy$) will itself be positive, and if you think about it the higher the correlation the greater the value of $\Sigma xy$.

When $X$ and $Y$ are negatively correlated however, high $X$ scores tend to be paired with low $Y$ scores (and vice-versa) which means that positive $X$ deviations pair with negative $Y$ deviations, leading to a negative cross-product. Similarly negative $X$ and positive $Y$ deviations tend to be paired with a resulting negative cross-product. So, for a negative correlation $\Sigma xy$ is itself negative. Similar reasoning suggests that with little or no correlation between $X$ and $Y$ the sum of the cross-products will tend toward zero.

So $\Sigma xy$ behaves in a way that we wish correlation coefficients to do, and all that remains is to ensure that the coefficient falls within the correct limits, i.e. maximum value of $+1$ and a minimum value of $-1$. The following formula accomplishes this:

$$\text{Pearson's r} = \frac{\Sigma xy}{\sqrt{(\Sigma x^2)(\Sigma y^2)}}$$

where $x = (X - \bar{X})$
and $y = (Y - \bar{Y})$

It is possible to test whether a Pearson's r correlation coefficient differs significantly from zero by using Table C.

## Step-by-step procedure

### Pearson's r

**Step 1** Having listed $X$ and $Y$ scores in pairs determine the means $\bar{X}$ and $\bar{Y}$

**Step 2** Determine the deviation scores ($x$) for $X$ by subtracting the mean ($\bar{X}$) from each score

**Step 3** Determine the deviation scores ($y$) for $Y$ by subtracting the mean ($\bar{Y}$) from each score

**Step 4** Square each $X$ deviation in turn and find their sum

**Step 5** Square each $Y$ deviation in turn and find their sum

**Step 6** Find $x \times y$ products for each pair of scores and find their sum

**Step 7** Find r by applying formula

$$r = \frac{\Sigma xy}{\sqrt{(\Sigma x^2)(\Sigma y^2)}}$$

**Step 8** If required, assess whether r differs significantly from zero by use of Table C.

**Step 9** Translate the results back in terms of the experiment

**Worked example**

## Pearson's r

| X | Y | Step 2 $x(= X - \bar{X})$ | Step 3 $y(= Y - \bar{Y})$ | $x^2$ | $y^2$ | $xy$ |
|---|---|---|---|---|---|---|
| 12 | 7 | +5 | −1·5 | 25 | 2·25 | −7·5 |
| 10 | 3 | +3 | −5·5 | 9 | 30·25 | −16·5 |
| 9 | 8 | +2 | −0·5 | 4 | 0·25 | −1·0 |
| 8 | 5 | +1 | −3·5 | 1 | 12·25 | −3·5 |
| 7 | 7 | 0 | −1·5 | 0 | 2·25 | 0 |
| 7 | 12 | 0 | +3·5 | 0 | 12·25 | 0 |
| 6 | 10 | −1 | +1·5 | 1 | 2·25 | −1·5 |
| 5 | 9 | −2 | +0·5 | 4 | 0·25 | −1·0 |
| 4 | 13 | −3 | +4·5 | 9 | 20·25 | −13·5 |
| 2 | 11 | −5 | +2·5 | 25 | 6·25 | −12·5 |

$\Sigma X = 70$  $\Sigma Y = 85$  $\Sigma x^2 = 78$  $\Sigma y^2 = 88·5$  $\Sigma xy = -57·0$

$\bar{X} = 7·0$  $\bar{Y} = 8·5$  **Step 4**  **Step 5**  **Step 6**

**Step 1**

**Step 7** $r = \dfrac{\Sigma xy}{\sqrt{(\Sigma x^2)(\Sigma y^2)}} = \dfrac{-57·0}{\sqrt{78 \times 88·5}} = -0·69$

**Step 8** From Table C, r must be greater than 0·53 for $N = 10$. As $r = -0·69$ the correlation between X and Y is significantly different from zero, at the $p = 0·05$ level

**Step 9** This would be expressed in terms of whatever X and Y represent, stressing that the correlation is negative and differs significantly from zero

# Appendix 3
# Statistical tables

## Table A Random numbers

```
03 47 43 73 86    36 96 47 36 61    46 98 63 71 62    33 26 16 80 45    60 11 14 10 95
97 74 24 67 62    42 81 14 57 20    42 53 32 37 32    27 07 36 07 51    24 51 79 89 73
16 76 62 27 66    56 50 26 71 07    32 90 79 78 53    13 55 38 58 59    88 97 54 14 10
12 56 85 99 26    96 96 68 27 31    05 03 72 93 15    57 12 10 14 21    88 26 49 81 76
55 59 56 35 64    38 54 82 46 22    31 62 43 09 90    06 18 44 32 53    23 83 01 30 30

16 22 77 94 39    49 54 43 54 82    17 37 93 23 78    87 35 20 96 43    84 26 34 91 64
84 42 17 53 31    57 24 55 06 88    77 04 74 47 67    21 76 33 50 25    83 92 12 06 76
63 01 63 78 59    16 95 55 67 19    98 10 50 71 75    12 86 73 58 07    44 39 52 38 79
33 21 12 34 29    78 64 56 07 82    52 42 07 44 38    15 51 00 13 42    99 66 02 79 54
57 60 86 32 44    09 47 27 96 54    49 17 46 09 62    90 52 84 77 27    08 02 73 43 28

18 18 07 92 46    44 17 16 58 09    79 83 86 19 62    06 76 50 03 10    55 23 64 05 05
26 62 38 97 75    84 16 07 44 99    83 11 46 32 24    20 14 85 88 45    10 93 72 88 71
23 42 40 64 74    82 97 77 77 81    07 45 32 14 08    32 98 94 07 72    93 85 79 10 75
52 36 28 19 95    50 92 26 11 97    00 56 76 31 38    80 22 02 53 53    86 60 42 04 53
37 85 94 35 12    83 39 50 08 30    42 34 07 96 88    54 42 06 87 98    35 85 29 48 39

70 29 17 12 13    40 33 20 38 26    13 89 51 03 74    17 76 37 13 04    07 74 21 19 30
56 62 18 37 35    96 83 50 87 75    97 12 25 93 47    70 33 24 03 54    97 77 46 44 80
99 49 57 22 77    88 42 95 45 72    16 64 36 16 00    04 43 18 66 79    94 77 24 21 90
16 08 15 04 72    33 27 14 34 90    45 59 34 68 49    12 72 07 34 45    99 27 72 95 14
31 16 93 32 43    50 27 89 87 19    20 15 37 00 49    52 85 66 60 44    38 68 88 11 80

68 34 30 13 70    55 74 30 77 40    44 22 78 84 26    04 33 46 09 52    68 07 97 06 57
74 57 35 65 76    59 29 97 68 60    71 91 38 67 54    13 58 18 24 76    15 54 55 95 52
27 42 37 86 53    48 55 90 65 72    96 57 69 36 10    96 46 92 42 45    97 60 49 04 91
00 39 68 29 61    66 37 32 20 30    77 84 57 03 29    10 45 65 04 26    11 04 96 67 24
29 94 98 94 24    68 49 69 10 82    53 75 91 93 30    34 25 20 57 27    40 48 73 51 92

16 90 82 66 59    83 62 64 11 12    67 19 00 71 74    60 47 21 29 68    02 02 37 03 31
11 27 94 75 06    06 09 19 74 66    02 94 37 34 02    76 70 90 30 86    38 45 94 30 38
35 24 10 16 20    33 32 51 26 38    79 78 45 04 91    16 92 53 56 16    02 75 50 95 98
38 23 16 86 38    42 38 97 01 50    87 75 66 81 41    40 01 74 91 62    48 51 84 08 32
31 96 25 91 47    96 44 33 49 13    34 86 82 53 91    00 52 43 48 85    27 55 26 89 62
```

# Table A Random numbers (continued)

```
66 67 40 67 14   64 05 71 95 86   11 05 65 09 68   76 83 20 37 90   57 16 00 11 66
14 90 84 45 11   75 73 88 05 90   52 27 41 14 86   22 98 12 22 08   07 52 74 95 80
68 05 51 18 00   33 96 02 75 19   07 60 62 93 55   59 33 82 43 90   49 37 38 44 59
20 46 78 73 90   97 51 40 14 02   04 02 33 31 08   39 54 16 49 36   47 95 93 13 30
64 19 58 97 79   15 06 15 93 20   01 09 10 75 06   40 78 78 89 62   02 67 74 17 33

05 26 93 70 60   22 35 85 15 13   92 03 51 59 77   59 56 78 06 83   52 91 05 70 74
07 97 10 88 23   09 98 42 99 64   61 71 62 99 15   06 51 29 16 93   58 05 77 09 51
68 71 86 85 85   54 87 66 47 54   73 32 08 11 12   44 95 92 63 16   29 56 24 29 48
26 99 61 65 53   58 37 78 80 70   42 10 50 67 42   32 17 55 85 74   94 44 67 19 94
14 65 52 68 75   87 59 36 22 41   26 78 63 06 55   13 08 27 01 50   15 29 39 39 43

17 53 77 58 71   71 41 61 50 72   12 41 94 96 26   44 95 27 36 99   02 96 74 30 83
90 26 59 21 19   23 52 23 33 12   96 93 02 18 39   07 02 18 36 07   25 99 32 70 23
41 23 52 55 99   31 04 49 69 96   10 47 48 45 88   13 41 43 89 20   97 17 14 49 17
60 20 50 81 69   31 99 73 68 68   35 81 33 03 76   24 30 12 48 60   18 99 10 72 34
91 25 38 05 90   94 58 28 41 36   45 37 59 03 09   90 35 57 29 12   82 62 54 65 60

34 50 57 74 37   98 80 33 00 91   09 77 93 19 82   74 94 80 04 04   45 07 31 66 49
85 22 04 39 43   73 81 53 94 79   33 62 46 86 28   08 31 54 46 31   53 94 13 38 47
09 79 13 77 48   73 82 97 22 21   05 03 27 24 83   72 89 44 05 60   35 80 39 94 88
88 75 80 18 14   22 95 75 42 49   39 32 82 22 49   02 48 07 70 37   16 04 61 67 87
90 96 23 70 00   39 00 03 06 90   55 85 78 38 36   94 37 30 69 32   90 89 00 76 33

53 74 23 99 67   61 32 28 69 84   94 62 67 86 24   98 33 41 19 95   47 53 53 38 09
63 38 06 86 54   99 00 65 26 94   02 82 90 23 07   79 62 67 80 60   75 91 12 81 19
35 30 58 21 46   06 72 17 10 94   25 21 31 75 96   49 28 24 00 49   55 65 79 78 07
63 43 36 82 69   65 51 18 37 88   61 38 44 12 45   32 92 85 88 65   54 34 81 85 35
98 25 37 55 26   01 91 82 81 46   74 71 12 94 97   24 02 71 37 07   03 92 18 66 75

02 63 21 17 69   71 50 80 89 56   38 15 70 11 48   43 40 45 86 98   00 83 26 91 03
64 55 22 21 82   48 22 28 06 00   61 54 13 43 91   82 78 12 23 29   06 66 24 12 27
85 07 26 13 89   01 10 07 82 04   59 63 69 36 03   69 11 15 83 80   13 29 54 19 28
58 54 16 24 15   51 54 44 82 00   62 61 65 04 69   38 18 65 18 97   85 72 13 49 21
34 85 27 84 87   61 48 64 56 26   90 18 48 13 26   37 70 15 42 57   65 65 80 39 07

03 92 18 27 46   57 99 16 96 56   30 33 72 85 22   84 64 38 56 98   99 01 30 98 64
62 95 30 27 59   37 75 41 66 48   86 97 80 61 45   23 53 04 01 63   45 76 08 64 27
08 45 93 15 22   60 21 75 46 91   98 77 27 85 42   28 88 61 08 84   69 62 03 42 73
07 08 55 18 40   45 44 75 13 90   24 94 96 61 02   57 55 66 83 15   73 42 37 11 61
01 85 89 95 66   51 10 19 34 88   15 84 97 19 75   12 76 39 43 78   64 63 91 08 25

72 84 71 14 35   19 11 58 49 26   50 11 17 17 76   86 31 57 20 18   95 60 78 46 75
88 78 28 16 84   13 52 53 94 53   75 45 69 30 96   73 89 65 70 31   99 17 43 48 76
45 17 75 65 57   28 40 19 72 12   25 12 74 75 67   60 40 60 81 19   24 62 01 61 16
96 76 28 12 54   22 01 11 94 25   71 96 16 16 88   68 64 36 74 45   19 59 50 88 92
43 31 67 72 30   24 02 94 08 63   38 32 36 66 02   69 36 38 25 39   48 03 45 15 22

50 44 66 44 21   66 06 58 05 62   68 15 54 35 02   42 35 48 96 32   14 52 41 52 48
22 66 22 14 86   26 63 75 41 99   58 42 36 72 24   58 37 52 18 51   03 37 18 39 11
96 24 40 14 51   23 22 30 88 57   95 67 47 29 83   94 69 40 06 07   18 16 36 78 86
31 73 91 61 19   60 20 72 93 48   98 57 07 23 69   65 95 39 69 58   56 80 30 19 44
78 70 73 99 84   43 89 94 36 45   56 69 47 07 41   90 22 91 07 12   78 35 34 08 72
```

| | | | | |
|---|---|---|---|---|
| 84 37 90 61 56 | 70 10 23 98 05 | 85 11 34 76 60 | 76 48 45 34 60 | 01 64 18 39 96 |
| 36 67 10 08 23 | 98 93 35 08 86 | 99 29 76 29 81 | 33 34 91 58 93 | 63 14 52 32 52 |
| 07 28 59 07 48 | 89 64 58 89 75 | 83 85 62 67 89 | 30 14 78 56 27 | 86 63 59 80 02 |
| 10 15 83 87 60 | 79 24 31 66 56 | 21 48 24 06 93 | 91 98 94 05 49 | 01 47 59 38 00 |
| 55 19 68 97 65 | 03 73 52 16 56 | 00 53 55 90 27 | 33 42 29 38 87 | 22 13 88 83 34 |
| | | | | |
| 53 81 29 13 39 | 35 01 20 71 34 | 62 33 74 82 14 | 53 73 19 09 03 | 56 54 29 56 93 |
| 51 86 32 68 92 | 33 98 74 66 99 | 40 14 71 94 58 | 45 94 19 38 81 | 14 44 99 81 07 |
| 35 91 70 29 13 | 80 03 54 07 27 | 96 94 78 32 66 | 50 95 52 74 33 | 13 80 55 62 54 |
| 37 71 67 95 13 | 20 02 44 95 94 | 64 85 04 05 72 | 01 32 90 76 14 | 53 89 74 60 41 |
| 93 66 13 83 27 | 92 79 64 64 72 | 28 54 96 53 84 | 48 14 52 98 94 | 56 07 93 89 30 |
| | | | | |
| 02 96 08 45 65 | 13 05 00 41 84 | 93 07 54 72 59 | 21 45 57 09 77 | 19 48 56 27 44 |
| 49 83 43 48 35 | 82 88 33 69 96 | 72 36 04 19 76 | 47 45 15 18 60 | 82 11 08 95 97 |
| 84 60 71 62 46 | 40 80 81 30 37 | 34 39 23 05 38 | 25 15 35 71 30 | 88 12 57 21 77 |
| 18 17 30 88 71 | 44 91 14 88 47 | 89 23 30 63 15 | 56 34 20 47 89 | 99 82 93 24 98 |
| 79 69 10 61 78 | 71 32 76 95 62 | 87 00 22 58 40 | 92 54 01 75 25 | 43 11 71 99 31 |
| | | | | |
| 75 93 36 57 83 | 56 20 14 82 11 | 74 21 97 90 65 | 96 42 68 63 86 | 74 54 13 26 94 |
| 38 30 92 29 03 | 06 28 81 39 38 | 62 25 06 84 63 | 61 29 08 93 67 | 04 32 92 08 09 |
| 51 29 50 10 34 | 31 57 75 95 80 | 51 97 02 74 77 | 76 15 48 49 44 | 18 55 63 77 09 |
| 21 31 38 86 24 | 37 79 81 53 74 | 73 24 16 10 33 | 52 83 90 94 76 | 70 47 14 54 36 |
| 29 01 23 87 88 | 58 02 39 37 67 | 42 10 14 20 92 | 16 55 23 42 45 | 54 96 09 11 06 |
| | | | | |
| 95 33 95 22 00 | 18 74 72 00 18 | 38 79 58 69 32 | 81 76 80 26 92 | 82 80 84 25 39 |
| 90 84 60 79 80 | 24 36 59 87 38 | 82 07 53 89 35 | 96 35 23 79 18 | 05 98 90 07 35 |
| 46 40 62 98 82 | 54 97 20 56 95 | 15 74 80 08 32 | 16 46 70 50 80 | 67 72 16 42 79 |
| 20 31 89 03 43 | 38 46 82 68 72 | 32 14 82 99 70 | 80 60 47 18 97 | 63 49 30 21 30 |
| 71 59 73 05 50 | 08 22 23 71 77 | 91 01 93 20 49 | 82 96 59 26 94 | 66 39 67 98 60 |

Abridged from Table 33 of R. A. Fisher and F. Yates, *Statistical Tables for Biological, Agricultural and Medical Research*, Oliver & Boyd Ltd, Edinburgh, 1953, by permission of the authors and publishers.

## Table B Sign test

$L$ = frequency of the less frequent sign
$T$ = total frequency of *both* pluses and minuses

The table gives the highest value of $L$ significant at the 0·05 level for each value of $T$ (two-tailed test)

| $T$ | $L$ |
|-----|-----|
| 5   | –   |
| 6   | 0   |
| 7   | 0   |
| 8   | 0   |
| 9   | 1   |
| 10  | 1   |
| 11  | 1   |
| 12  | 2   |
| 13  | 2   |
| 14  | 2   |
| 15  | 3   |
| 16  | 3   |
| 17  | 3   |
| 18  | 4   |
| 19  | 4   |
| 20  | 5   |
| 21  | 5   |
| 22  | 5   |
| 23  | 6   |
| 24  | 6   |
| 25  | 7   |

## Table C Significance of correlation coefficients
(Spearman's rho and Pearson's r)

$N$ = number of pairs of scores

The table values are the smallest values of correlation coefficient significantly different from zero at the 0·05 level for different values of $N$ (one-tailed test).
For $N$ greater than 10 the value needed for significance is essentially the same for either test.

| $N$ | Spearman's rho | Pearson's r | $N$ | Spearman's rho or Pearson's r |
|-----|----------------|-------------|-----|-------------------------------|
| 5   | 0·90           | 0·81        | 11  | 0·52                          |
| 6   | 0·83           | 0·73        | 12  | 0·50                          |
| 7   | 0·71           | 0·67        | 13  | 0·48                          |
| 8   | 0·64           | 0·62        | 14  | 0·46                          |
| 9   | 0·60           | 0·58        | 15  | 0·44                          |
| 10  | 0·56           | 0·55        | 16  | 0·43                          |
|     |                |             | 17  | 0·41                          |
|     |                |             | 18  | 0·40                          |
|     |                |             | 19  | 0·39                          |
|     |                |             | 20  | 0·38                          |
|     |                |             | 21  | 0·37                          |
|     |                |             | 22  | 0·36                          |
|     |                |             | 23  | 0·35                          |
|     |                |             | 24  | 0·34                          |
|     |                |             | 25  | 0·34                          |
|     |                |             | 26  | 0·33                          |
|     |                |             | 27  | 0·32                          |
|     |                |             | 28  | 0·32                          |
|     |                |             | 29  | 0·31                          |
|     |                |             | 30  | 0·31                          |

*Note* For $N$ greater than 30 the value needed for significance can be taken as 0·31

## Table D The normal distribution

Fractional area under the standard normal curve from 0 to $z$

| z | 0 | 1 | 2 | 3 | 4 | 5 | 6 | 7 | 8 | 9 |
|---|---|---|---|---|---|---|---|---|---|---|
| 0·0 | ·0000 | ·0040 | ·0080 | ·0120 | ·0160 | ·0199 | ·0239 | ·0279 | ·0319 | ·0359 |
| 0·1 | ·0398 | ·0438 | ·0478 | ·0517 | ·0557 | ·0596 | ·0636 | ·0675 | ·0714 | ·0754 |
| 0·2 | ·0793 | ·0832 | ·0871 | ·0910 | ·0948 | ·0987 | ·1026 | ·1064 | ·1103 | ·1141 |
| 0·3 | ·1179 | ·1217 | ·1255 | ·1293 | ·1331 | ·1368 | ·1406 | ·1443 | ·1480 | ·1517 |
| 0·4 | ·1554 | ·1591 | ·1628 | ·1664 | ·1736 | ·1700 | ·1772 | ·1808 | ·1844 | ·1879 |
| 0·5 | ·1915 | ·1950 | ·1985 | ·2019 | ·2054 | ·2088 | ·2123 | ·2157 | ·2190 | ·2224 |
| 0·6 | ·2258 | ·2291 | ·2324 | ·2357 | ·2389 | ·2422 | ·2454 | ·2486 | ·2518 | ·2549 |
| 0·7 | ·2580 | ·2612 | ·2642 | ·2673 | ·2704 | ·2734 | ·2764 | ·2794 | ·2823 | ·2852 |
| 0·8 | ·2881 | ·2910 | ·2939 | ·2967 | ·2996 | ·3023 | ·3051 | ·3078 | ·3106 | ·3133 |
| 0·9 | ·3159 | ·3186 | ·3212 | ·3238 | ·3264 | ·3289 | ·3315 | ·3340 | ·3365 | ·3389 |
| 1·0 | ·3413 | ·3438 | ·3461 | ·3485 | ·3508 | ·3531 | ·3554 | ·3577 | ·3599 | ·3621 |
| 1·1 | ·3643 | ·3665 | ·3686 | ·3708 | ·3729 | ·3749 | ·3770 | ·3790 | ·3810 | ·3830 |
| 1·2 | ·3849 | ·3869 | ·3888 | ·3907 | ·3925 | ·3944 | ·3962 | ·3980 | ·3997 | ·4015 |
| 1·3 | ·4032 | ·4049 | ·4066 | ·4082 | ·4099 | ·4115 | ·4131 | ·4147 | ·4162 | ·4177 |
| 1·4 | ·4192 | ·4297 | ·4222 | ·4236 | ·4251 | ·4265 | ·4279 | ·4292 | ·4306 | ·4319 |
| 1·5 | ·4332 | ·4345 | ·4357 | ·4370 | ·4382 | ·4394 | ·4406 | ·4418 | ·4429 | ·4441 |
| 1·6 | ·4452 | ·4463 | ·4474 | ·4484 | ·4495 | ·4505 | ·4515 | ·4525 | ·4535 | ·4545 |
| 1·7 | ·4554 | ·4564 | ·4573 | ·4582 | ·4591 | ·4599 | ·4608 | ·4625 | ·4625 | ·4633 |
| 1·8 | ·4641 | ·4649 | ·4656 | ·4664 | ·4671 | ·4678 | ·4686 | ·4699 | ·4699 | ·4706 |
| 1·9 | ·4713 | ·4719 | ·4726 | ·4732 | ·4738 | ·4744 | ·4750 | ·4761 | ·4761 | ·4767 |
| 2·0 | ·4772 | ·4778 | ·4783 | ·4788 | ·4793 | ·4798 | ·4803 | ·4808 | ·4812 | ·4817 |
| 2·1 | ·4821 | ·4826 | ·4830 | ·4834 | ·4838 | ·4842 | ·4846 | ·4850 | ·4854 | ·4857 |
| 2·2 | ·4861 | ·4864 | ·4868 | ·4871 | ·4875 | ·4878 | ·4881 | ·4884 | ·4887 | ·4890 |
| 2·3 | ·4893 | ·4896 | ·4898 | ·4901 | ·4904 | ·4906 | ·4909 | ·4911 | ·4913 | ·4916 |
| 2·4 | ·4918 | ·4920 | ·4922 | ·4925 | ·4927 | ·4929 | ·4931 | ·4932 | ·4934 | ·4936 |
| 2·5 | ·4938 | ·4940 | ·4941 | ·4943 | ·4945 | ·4946 | ·4948 | ·4949 | ·4951 | ·4952 |
| 2·6 | ·4953 | ·4955 | ·4956 | ·4957 | ·4959 | ·4960 | ·4961 | ·4962 | ·4963 | ·4964 |
| 2·7 | ·4965 | ·4966 | ·4967 | ·4968 | ·4969 | ·4970 | ·4871 | ·4972 | ·4973 | ·4974 |
| 2·8 | ·4974 | ·4975 | ·4976 | ·4977 | ·4977 | ·4978 | ·4979 | ·4979 | ·4980 | ·4981 |
| 2·9 | ·4981 | ·4982 | ·4982 | ·4983 | ·4984 | ·4984 | ·4985 | ·4985 | ·4986 | ·4986 |
| 3·0 | ·4987 | ·4987 | ·4987 | ·4988 | ·4988 | ·4989 | ·4989 | ·4989 | ·4990 | ·4990 |
| 3·1 | ·4990 | ·4991 | ·4991 | ·4991 | ·4992 | ·4992 | ·4992 | ·4992 | ·4992 | ·4993 |
| 3·2 | ·4993 | ·4993 | ·4994 | ·4994 | ·4994 | ·4994 | ·4994 | ·4995 | ·4995 | ·4995 |
| 3·3 | ·4995 | ·4995 | ·4995 | ·4996 | ·4996 | ·4996 | ·4996 | ·4996 | ·4996 | ·4997 |
| 3·4 | ·4997 | ·4997 | ·4997 | ·4997 | ·4997 | ·4997 | ·4997 | ·4997 | ·4997 | ·4998 |
| 3·5 | ·4998 | ·4998 | ·4998 | ·4998 | ·4998 | ·4998 | ·4998 | ·4998 | ·4998 | ·4998 |
| 3·6 | ·4998 | ·4998 | ·4999 | ·4999 | ·4999 | ·4999 | ·4999 | ·4999 | ·4999 | ·4999 |
| 3·7 | ·4999 | ·4999 | ·4999 | ·4999 | ·4999 | ·4999 | ·4999 | ·4999 | ·4999 | ·4999 |
| 3·8 | ·4999 | ·4999 | ·4999 | ·4999 | ·4999 | ·4999 | ·4999 | ·4999 | ·4999 | ·4999 |
| 3·9 | ·5000 | ·5000 | ·5000 | ·5000 | ·5000 | ·5000 | ·5000 | ·5000 | ·5000 | ·5000 |

## Table E The *t*-distribution

(5 per cent significance level for two-tailed test)

| d.f. | *t* |
|------|--------|
| 1 | 12·706 |
| 2 | 4·303 |
| 3 | 3·182 |
| 4 | 2·776 |
| 5 | 2·571 |
| 6 | 2·447 |
| 7 | 2·365 |
| 8 | 2·306 |
| 9 | 2·262 |
| 10 | 2·228 |
| 11 | 2·201 |
| 12 | 2·179 |
| 13 | 2·160 |
| 14 | 2·145 |
| 15 | 2·131 |
| 16 | 2·120 |
| 17 | 2·110 |
| 18 | 2·101 |
| 19 | 2·093 |
| 20 | 2·086 |
| 21 | 2·080 |
| 22 | 2·074 |
| 23 | 2·069 |
| 24 | 2·064 |
| 25 | 2·060 |
| 26 | 2·056 |
| 27 | 2·052 |
| 28 | 2·048 |
| 29 | 2·045 |
| 30 | 2·042 |
| 40 | 2·021 |
| 60 | 2·000 |
| 120 | 1·980 |
| ∞ | 1·960 |

Abridged from Table 12 of E. S. Pearson and H. O. Hartley, *Biometrika Tables for Statisticians*, vol. 1, Cambridge University Press, 1954.

# Table F The variance ratio (F)

(5 per cent significance level for two-tailed test)

$N_1$ are the degrees of freedom for greater variance   $N_2$ are the degrees of freedom for smaller variance

| $N_1 =$ | 1 | 2 | 3 | 4 | 5 | 6 | 7 | 8 | 9 | 10 | 12 | 15 | 20 | 24 | 30 | 40 | 60 | 120 | x |
|---|---|---|---|---|---|---|---|---|---|---|---|---|---|---|---|---|---|---|---|
| $N_2 =$ 1 | 648 | 800 | 864 | 900 | 922 | 937 | 948 | 957 | 963 | 969 | 977 | 985 | 993 | 997 | 1001 | 1006 | 1010 | 1014 | 1018 |
| 2 | 38.51 | 39.00 | 39.16 | 39.25 | 39.30 | 39.33 | 39.36 | 39.37 | 39.39 | 39.40 | 39.42 | 39.43 | 39.45 | 39.46 | 39.46 | 39.47 | 39.48 | 39.49 | 39.50 |
| 3 | 17.44 | 16.04 | 15.44 | 15.10 | 14.88 | 14.74 | 14.62 | 14.54 | 14.47 | 14.42 | 14.34 | 14.25 | 14.17 | 14.12 | 14.08 | 14.04 | 13.99 | 13.95 | 13.90 |
| 4 | 12.22 | 10.65 | 9.98 | 9.60 | 9.36 | 9.20 | 9.07 | 8.98 | 8.90 | 8.84 | 8.75 | 8.66 | 8.56 | 8.51 | 8.46 | 8.41 | 8.36 | 8.31 | 8.26 |
| 5 | 10.01 | 8.43 | 7.76 | 7.39 | 7.15 | 6.98 | 6.85 | 6.76 | 6.68 | 6.62 | 6.52 | 6.43 | 6.33 | 6.28 | 6.23 | 6.18 | 6.12 | 6.07 | 6.02 |
| 6 | 8.81 | 7.26 | 6.60 | 6.23 | 5.99 | 5.82 | 5.70 | 5.60 | 5.52 | 5.46 | 5.37 | 5.27 | 5.17 | 5.12 | 5.07 | 5.01 | 4.96 | 4.90 | 4.85 |
| 7 | 8.07 | 6.54 | 5.89 | 5.52 | 5.29 | 5.12 | 4.99 | 4.90 | 4.82 | 4.76 | 4.67 | 4.57 | 4.47 | 4.42 | 4.36 | 4.31 | 4.25 | 4.20 | 4.14 |
| 8 | 7.57 | 6.06 | 5.42 | 5.05 | 4.82 | 4.65 | 4.53 | 4.43 | 4.36 | 4.30 | 4.20 | 4.10 | 4.00 | 3.95 | 3.89 | 3.84 | 3.78 | 3.73 | 3.67 |
| 9 | 7.21 | 5.71 | 5.08 | 4.72 | 4.48 | 4.32 | 4.20 | 4.10 | 4.03 | 3.96 | 3.87 | 3.77 | 3.67 | 3.61 | 3.56 | 3.51 | 3.45 | 3.39 | 3.33 |
| 10 | 6.94 | 5.46 | 4.83 | 4.47 | 4.24 | 4.07 | 3.95 | 3.85 | 3.78 | 3.72 | 3.62 | 3.52 | 3.42 | 3.37 | 3.31 | 3.26 | 3.20 | 3.14 | 3.08 |
| 11 | 6.55 | 5.10 | 4.47 | 4.12 | 3.89 | 3.73 | 3.61 | 3.51 | 3.44 | 3.37 | 3.28 | 3.18 | 3.07 | 3.02 | 2.96 | 2.91 | 2.85 | 2.79 | 2.72 |
| 13 | 6.20 | 4.76 | 4.15 | 3.80 | 3.58 | 3.41 | 3.29 | 3.20 | 3.12 | 3.06 | 2.96 | 2.86 | 2.76 | 2.70 | 2.64 | 2.58 | 2.52 | 2.46 | 2.40 |
| 20 | 5.87 | 4.46 | 3.86 | 3.51 | 3.29 | 3.13 | 3.01 | 2.91 | 2.84 | 2.77 | 2.68 | 2.57 | 2.46 | 2.41 | 2.35 | 2.29 | 2.22 | 2.16 | 2.09 |
| 24 | 5.72 | 4.32 | 3.72 | 3.38 | 3.15 | 2.99 | 2.87 | 2.78 | 2.70 | 2.64 | 2.54 | 2.44 | 2.33 | 2.27 | 2.21 | 2.15 | 2.08 | 2.01 | 1.94 |
| 30 | 5.57 | 4.18 | 3.59 | 3.25 | 3.03 | 2.87 | 2.75 | 2.65 | 2.57 | 2.51 | 2.41 | 2.31 | 2.20 | 2.14 | 2.07 | 2.01 | 1.94 | 1.87 | 1.79 |
| 40 | 5.42 | 4.05 | 3.46 | 3.13 | 2.90 | 2.74 | 2.62 | 2.53 | 2.45 | 2.39 | 2.29 | 2.18 | 2.07 | 2.01 | 1.94 | 1.88 | 1.80 | 1.72 | 1.64 |
| 60 | 5.29 | 3.93 | 3.34 | 3.01 | 2.79 | 2.63 | 2.51 | 2.41 | 2.33 | 2.27 | 2.17 | 2.06 | 1.94 | 1.88 | 1.82 | 1.74 | 1.67 | 1.58 | 1.48 |
| 120 | 5.15 | 3.80 | 3.23 | 2.89 | 2.67 | 2.52 | 2.39 | 2.30 | 2.22 | 2.16 | 2.05 | 1.94 | 1.82 | 1.76 | 1.69 | 1.61 | 1.53 | 1.43 | 1.31 |
| x | 5.02 | 3.69 | 3.12 | 2.79 | 2.57 | 2.41 | 2.29 | 2.19 | 2.11 | 2.05 | 1.94 | 1.83 | 1.71 | 1.64 | 1.57 | 1.48 | 1.39 | 1.27 | 1.00 |

Abridged from M. Merrington and C. M. Thompson, 'Tables of percentage points of the inverted beta (F) distribution'. *Biometrika*, vol. 33, 1943, pp. 73–8.

## Table G Chi square

(5 per cent significance level for one-tailed test)

| d.f. | $\chi^2$ |
|------|----------|
| 1 | 3·841 |
| 2 | 5·991 |
| 3 | 7·815 |
| 4 | 9·488 |
| 5 | 11·071 |
| 6 | 12·592 |
| 7 | 14·067 |
| 8 | 15·507 |
| 9 | 16·919 |
| 10 | 18·307 |
| 11 | 19·675 |
| 12 | 21·026 |
| 13 | 22·362 |
| 14 | 23·685 |
| 15 | 24·996 |
| 16 | 26·296 |
| 17 | 27·587 |
| 18 | 28·869 |
| 19 | 30·144 |
| 20 | 31·410 |
| 21 | 32·671 |
| 22 | 33·924 |
| 23 | 35·173 |
| 24 | 36·415 |
| 25 | 37·653 |
| 26 | 38·885 |
| 27 | 40·113 |
| 28 | 41·337 |
| 29 | 42·557 |
| 30 | 43·773 |
| 40 | 55·759 |
| 50 | 67·505 |
| 60 | 79·082 |
| 80 | 101·879 |
| 100 | 124·342 |

Abridged from Table 8 of E. S. Pearson and H. O. Hartley, *Biometrika Tables for Statisticians*, vol. 1, Cambridge University Press, 1954.

## Table H Mann-Whitney test

(5 per cent significance level for two-tailed test)

| $N_B =$ | 4 | 5 | 6 | 7 | 8 |
|---|---|---|---|---|---|
| $N_A = 2$ | — | — | — | — | 0 |
| 3 | — | 0 | 1 | 1 | 2 |
| 4 | 0 | 1 | 2 | 3 | 4 |
| 5 | — | 2 | 3 | 5 | 6 |
| 6 | — | — | 5 | 6 | 8 |
| 7 | — | — | — | 8 | 10 |
| 8 | — | — | — | — | 13 |

Adapted and abridged from H. B. Mann and D. R. Whitney, 'On a test of whether one of two random variables is stochastically larger than the other', *Annals of Mathematical Statistics*, vol. 18, 1947, pp. 52–4.

| $N_B =$ | 9 | 10 | 11 | 12 | 13 | 14 | 15 | 16 | 17 | 18 | 19 | 20 |
|---|---|---|---|---|---|---|---|---|---|---|---|---|
| $N_A = 1$ | | | | | | | | | | | | |
| 2 | 0 | 0 | 0 | 1 | 1 | 1 | 1 | 1 | 2 | 2 | 2 | 2 |
| 3 | 2 | 3 | 3 | 4 | 4 | 5 | 5 | 6 | 6 | 7 | 7 | 8 |
| 4 | 4 | 5 | 6 | 7 | 8 | 9 | 10 | 11 | 11 | 12 | 13 | 13 |
| 5 | 7 | 8 | 9 | 11 | 12 | 13 | 14 | 15 | 17 | 18 | 19 | 20 |
| 6 | 10 | 11 | 13 | 14 | 16 | 17 | 19 | 21 | 22 | 24 | 25 | 27 |
| 7 | 12 | 14 | 16 | 18 | 20 | 22 | 24 | 26 | 28 | 30 | 32 | 34 |
| 8 | 15 | 17 | 19 | 22 | 24 | 26 | 29 | 31 | 34 | 36 | 38 | 41 |
| 9 | 17 | 20 | 23 | 26 | 28 | 31 | 34 | 37 | 39 | 42 | 45 | 48 |
| 10 | 20 | 23 | 26 | 29 | 33 | 36 | 39 | 42 | 45 | 48 | 52 | 55 |
| 11 | 23 | 26 | 30 | 33 | 37 | 40 | 44 | 47 | 51 | 55 | 58 | 62 |
| 12 | 26 | 29 | 33 | 37 | 41 | 45 | 49 | 53 | 57 | 61 | 65 | 69 |
| 13 | 28 | 33 | 37 | 41 | 45 | 50 | 54 | 59 | 63 | 67 | 72 | 76 |
| 14 | 31 | 36 | 40 | 45 | 50 | 54 | 59 | 64 | 67 | 74 | 78 | 83 |
| 15 | 34 | 39 | 44 | 49 | 54 | 59 | 64 | 70 | 75 | 80 | 85 | 90 |
| 16 | 37 | 42 | 47 | 53 | 59 | 63 | 70 | 75 | 81 | 86 | 92 | 98 |
| 17 | 39 | 45 | 51 | 57 | 63 | 67 | 75 | 81 | 87 | 93 | 99 | 105 |
| 18 | 42 | 48 | 55 | 61 | 67 | 74 | 80 | 86 | 93 | 99 | 106 | 112 |
| 19 | 45 | 52 | 58 | 65 | 72 | 78 | 85 | 92 | 99 | 106 | 113 | 119 |
| 20 | 48 | 55 | 62 | 69 | 76 | 83 | 90 | 98 | 105 | 112 | 119 | 127 |

Adapted and abridged from Tables 1, 3, 5 and 7 of D. Aube, 'Extended tables for the Mann-Whitney statistic', *Bulletin of the Institute of Educational Research at Indiana University*, vol. 1, 1953, no. 2.

## Table J Wilcoxon test

(5 per cent significance for two-tailed test)

| $N$ | $T$ |
|-----|-----|
| 6 | 1 |
| 7 | 2 |
| 8 | 4 |
| 9 | 6 |
| 10 | 8 |
| 11 | 11 |
| 12 | 14 |
| 13 | 17 |
| 14 | 21 |
| 15 | 25 |
| 16 | 30 |
| 17 | 35 |
| 18 | 40 |
| 19 | 46 |
| 20 | 52 |
| 21 | 59 |
| 22 | 66 |
| 23 | 73 |
| 24 | 81 |
| 25 | 90 |

Adapted from Table 2 of F. Wilcoxon and R. A. Wilcox,
*Some Rapid Approximate Statistical Procedures*, American Cyanamid Company,
1964.

# Index